John -

It's one of my
greatest honors
to be able to

help another man
realize his vision
and live out his
purpose. Thank you
for allowing me
to join your journey.

Jonathan Dawson

Published by Waymaker Learning Corporation, Florence, South Carolina

ISBN: 978-0-9911309-0-0

This publication is designed to provide educational information. It is sold with the understanding that publisher is not engaged in rendering legal or accounting advice. If such advice or assistance is required, the services of a competent professional should be sought.

The opinions expressed by the authors in this book are not endorsed by Waymaker Learning Corporation and are the sole responsibility of the author rendering the opinion.

For more information, please write:
Waymaker Learning Corporation
1082 Greenview Drive
Florence, South Carolina 29501

Visit us online at: waymakerlearningcorporation.com

Cover and Interior Design: Candesign Creative Design and Multimedia
www.candesignonline.com

Editorial Support: Bridgette Coates

Printed in the USA by Signature Book Printing, www.sbpbooks.com

RACE TO THE

FINISH LINE

GAINING AND RETAINING
YOUR COMPETITIVE ADVANTAGE

Preface

Gathering the right tools and the right team are essential to building a winning team. In business, getting to the finish line is an accomplishment, but standing in the "Winner's Circle" is the ultimate thrill of victory.

In our first book in this *Race to The Finish Line* series, we focused on getting you started in business. In this sequel version, or volume two, if you will, we have assembled a team of experts to help you take your business to the next level, to a place where standing in the Winner's Circle is commonplace.

Champions in sports, and certainly in business, develop a skill set that the competition has a hard time replicating. They learn and develop their craft so as to distinguish themselves from others in the marketplace. A critical component of the champion's strategy is to not only get to the top, but to stay there for decades or even generations.

So then, prepare yourself to take a ride in the pace car with us as we travel around the track and learn from some of the best! Get ready for a fantastic trip! You will want to be observant as you read. Glean from each page the sage counsel provided by the winners who have contributed to this work.

So as they say on race day…"Gentleman, start your engines."

Table of Contents

Dedication

At the time of publication, the authors of this book are acutely aware of the volatility of the world in which we live. To pursue a business endeavor in our great nation is truly a privilege and a blessing.

Therefore, it is with great respect and gratitude that we dedicate the pages of this work to the brave men and women of the United States Armed Forces, law enforcement officers and emergency personnel from across this nation. Your daily heroic efforts to protect our freedoms at home and abroad give each of us confidence in tomorrow. Your duty calls you, but your commitment keeps you in the fight to provide a safe place for all of us to live and work. While your efforts may go unnoticed by some, we salute you and thank you!

May God bless you and this Great Nation!

INTRODUCTION

Do you ever wonder how some of the best companies, businesses and/or dealerships with whom you do business survive? Many of them, to the amazement of other similar organizations, not only survive but thrive in the good and the bad times. The answers in every situation are not the same, nor are they always easy to explain.

However, it is very likely that in a lot of these businesses and firms you will find distinctive differences. The products may be similar, but the service is exponentially different. The service may be touted to be the same, but the actual delivery of service is clearly not the same. The distribution systems of some are efficient, but not quick. While others get the product to you quickly, often times it is not the correct product. And then, of course, there is the issue of cost or price for the product or service. Many companies try to distinguish themselves as the low cost provider while tacking on loads of hidden fees. Others clearly state "we are great, but we ain't cheap".

Where is the parody? How does a consumer determine which company and/or product is best for them? How does the company consistently position itself as the best option and deliver on that promise over and over again?

All of these are the kinds of questions that businesses need to address if they are going to win the race. If we had a crystal ball and could see into the future, we would be able to take the short cut to the winner's circle by outpacing our competition without the need to create and hold onto a competitive advantage. Taking a position on the track is not the same as holding first position throughout the majority of the race and into the checkered flag on the last lap!

In *Race to The Finish Line…Gaining and Retaining Your Competitive Advantage*, we have attempted to answer many of the questions businesses, new and old, must address if they are to thrive in today's competitive marketplace. Our team of authors will address how to clarify your competitive advantage, as well as, the impact technology plays in your business and how to maximize it. We will explore new and creative ways to provide customer assurance and improve satisfaction by employing reinsurance programs.

In this book, you will learn from industry leaders in sales, customer service and relationship management. You will get advice from media experts and training pros on how to set your business apart and move your entire team closer to the winner's circle.

Our pit crew of authors includes some veteran returning authors, as well as, some rookie team members. All of the crew are gifted and experienced in their respective fields. This list includes Dave Villa, CEO of Imperial Press Direct; David Cribbs, Lead Trainer with Auto Dealer University; Tim Byrd, President of Dealer RE; Jason Reaves, President of Wayne Reaves Computer Systems, Inc.; Jonathan Dawson, Founder and CEO of LITE Consulting, Inc; Chip Cooper, President of Comsoft, Inc.; Michael Samaan, Director of Sales for Auto Data Direct, Inc.; John Brown, Executive Director of CIADA; and Marty Coates, Co-Founder, Waymaker Learning Corporation.

Among the topics to be discussed are:

1- Determining your competitive advantage

2- Increasing your competitive place by understanding and implementing sales strategies

3- Increasing your commitment to customers by providing your own protection system

4- Getting to "HOW"

5- Building relationships with your customers differently than the competition

6- Using technology to beat your competition

In this second book of the *Race to The Finish Line* series, we aim for you to gather great content in an easy-to-read format. We encourage you to use the space provided in the book to take notes. Make this book a tool by listing your own questions, jotting answers to questions and making plans to determine and ingrain your competitive advantage into your business culture. And as you develop a comfort level with one or more of the authors, use the contact information provided herein to contact them. The authors of this book are providing this material while earning no royalties and providing most of the profit from the book to a non-profit organization. They are in business themselves to make a profit, but they also believe passionately about leading others to success while creating opportunities of success for their business.

It is our pleasure to invite you now to get started in your quest to gain and retain a competitive advantage. You will not need a racing helmet or even your car just yet. But grab a pen, your reading glasses, if necessary, and plunge into the pages of this terrific read. We all look forward to seeing you and your team in the Winner's Circle!!

CHAPTER ONE
In Quest of The ExtraOrdinary...
Your Competitive Advantage
By Marty Coates

Some years ago, a potential business client invited me to dinner at one of my favorite restaurants, The Angus Barn. A dinner meeting after an already full day of platform speaking demands a great place for conversation, atmosphere, great food, and most importantly, terrific service. My expectations for all the above were high as I choose this venue whenever I am in the Raleigh area and circumstances allow.

Upon arrival at exactly 7:15 pm, I met my party and very quickly our table was ready. The hostess seated us and indicated that our server would be by in just a minute.

Almost to the exact projected time, our server arrived. Immediately I noticed in the way she greeted us and asked questions about our desires for beverages and the menu, that she was no rookie.

After being treated royally for a couple of hours over dinner, I asked Yvonne, the server, a couple of questions. First, I asked her how long she had worked at The Angus Barn. To my surprise, she said with enthusiasm, "thirty-three years!" "Wow," I said, "that is a really long time in any business, but especially in the food and restaurant business." She acknowledged as much, but was quick to retort and say, "but I have a colleague who has worked here forty-nine years." "What? Are you kidding me?" I replied. Neither Yvonne nor her colleague was related to the family that owns Angus Barn.

Encouragingly and seriously I asked Yvonne why she had worked there so long. She responded with no delay, "Because they love me here." At first I thought she meant the management staff. While she affirmed that, she went on to say, she mostly meant the customers. And she added, "I love them, too."

What makes this story ExtraOrdinary is this. Yvonne and others who stay at an establishment of this caliber are paid above average tips and earn a decent living. But it was clear to me, even before she told me, Yvonne did not work at The Angus Barn because of the money or the benefits. In fact, she works there because of LOVE. She loves her co-workers, managers, supervisors and owners and she knows they love her. She loves her customers and they love her. That understanding of purpose and her self-inspired passion to serve gives her energy and drives her to action on behalf of her customers.

Before we left, I thought I would try to get contact information from her so I could send a note to her manager to recognize her great service to us. Thinking it was a long shot, I asked, "Do you have a business card?" Without hesitation she retrieved from her apron a business card with her name on it and below that, her title. It simply read…SERVER. How appropriate. She proudly claims her restaurant and her title.

The real message behind this story, the history of one fantastic place and terrific employee, is the ExtraOrdinary Competitive Advantage. The Angus Barn has it. Customers pay more and do not mind waiting for their date on the calendar to get the table they want. While there are countless other restaurants in Raleigh that offer great service and good food, they are not this place. The ambiance of the library, the Wild Turkey Lounge, or the behind the scenes table-for-two in the kitchen where guests can watch the full kitchen in action and enjoy their personal meal prepared by a chef are all unique. So many other amenities are offered and to cap it off, as each guest leaves, a barrel of fresh North Carolina apples are there for the taking. Yes, competitive advantage is the secret ingredient that has placed this restaurant experience at the top of the list for regulars, tourists, and occasional guests.

So then, what is Competitive Advantage? How does a company gain it and then hang on to it for decades? This question goes to the very core of your business. Your aim is to determine what makes you different from other businesses.

While there are a number of theories and opinions on the exact nature of competitive advantage, I explain it simply as what you are better at than your competition. An organization may get there by traveling any number of avenues, however, the best approach is to first do some soul searching. Matt Wilson, co-founder of Under30CEO.com, described this process in his article, "Three Steps to Gain a Competitive Advantage," as "going on a treasure hunt to find an underserved niche". For established firms, dealerships, or businesses this may seem trite. But that very feeling could be the reason you need to look further to determine the "what" before engaging in the "how". What makes you, your company, your service or your product ExtraOrdinary?

As a matter of definition let's say that ExtraOrdinary means *very unusual or exemplary, phenomenal, astonishing, sensational, incredible or unbelievable.* If you could with some confidence claim or retain that kind of reputation in your marketplace, would that not give you a superior position over your competition?

Begin by asking some really important questions about your business and product.
For example:

1) Does the product or service you sell and/or provide address a particular customer or market need?
2) Who are your customers and how can your product or service help them?
3) What other companies seek to provide the same thing?
4) Is your product or service unique in any way? If so, how?
5) How can you make your product stand out among similar products?
6) What is it about your product or service that is ExtraOrdinary?

With the answers to these or other similar questions, presumably you can start on a path to determining your competitive advantage.

The modern era's tried and true methods of determining competitive advantage are normally accomplished by examining three different primary categories in your business. Michael Porter, renowned theorist and Harvard Professor, is credited with having the broadest and best approach. He suggests that a company should explore these areas:
1) Cost Leadership;
2) Differentiation; and
3) Alliances.

Cost Leadership

This is the first area in which many companies will attempt to gain an advantage. By offering a similar product or service for a lesser price, they hope to position themselves ahead of the competition in the minds of the buyer. It could certainly be advantageous to produce and distribute a product or service at a lesser cost and then offer it to the end user at a lesser price; however, this position can be extremely difficult to maintain as market forces directly impact costs. Normally this is considered an offensive tactic designed to drive competition out of the marketplace by winning over customers on price. Even when it is successful it requires constant adjustments as new competitors enter the market, thus requiring new price strategies to hold a competitive advantage.

Car manufacturer, Toyota, claimed its market position using this tactic years ago. By providing a quality product at a considerably lower price point than its U.S. based competitors, it gained advantage and has held onto it now for decades. Despite challenges in recent years with safety recalls on many of its models, Toyota has combined quality and price to retain its place as a top candidate for many potential car buyers.

Differentiation

This is the second strategy that you can use to set your company apart from your competitors. Differentiation strategies allow you to show distinct differences to your customers in any number of areas in the company or in the attributes of your product or service. Low cost is one attribute to consider, but you may also look at service, quality, personnel, the location of the business/dealership, speed of delivery, knowledge base and/or unique characteristics. Identify one or more of these attributes and then find the right market segments to which to market these differences.

Alliances

An effective way to gain advantage is by strategic alliances with other businesses in related industries or fields. This strategy can be employed, but companies must be careful not to do so in an attempt to control price. As long as you do not cross the line, a company can partner with other companies to pool resources and share costs. In doing so, your company may gain exposure at the expense of other competitors not in the alliance.

Most companies find that sub-differentiation is where the real advantage lies. In many industries today, a unique idea is quickly copied. The time it takes to get a product to market is often reduced with the use of technological advances. Except for the burdensome hassle of local, state and federal government red tape, what is unique today will be commonplace tomorrow. How then does one organization get to this advantage spot?

ExtraOrdinary Competitive Advantage is the point at which you drill down further to determine your real uniqueness. Consider your customer service, your technology platforms, your communication with your customers, your brand awareness among your customers, your key personnel, your quality, and most of all, the experience of doing business with you.

I have long contended that it is in the "little things" that we separate ourselves from our competitors. Paying attention to the details makes a world of difference when something goes wrong. But it is just as important during the normal course of business each day.

A recent change in pricing strategy at Walt Disney Parks is sure to raise some eyebrows. Disney now will charge customers based on when they want to come to the park. It will cost more during high traffic times like spring break, the summer months and Christmas holidays. For annual pass holders in Florida, that could mean paying more for exclusive access or settling for passes with blackout periods. Why would Disney make such a decision? Their customer feedback indicated that the customer wanted to be able to come at certain times and would pay more to do so, and when the lines are so long that they cannot enjoy their time here, they will try other parks. The customers meant that it is not the park they come for, but for the "ExtraOrdinary Experience". Walt Disney knew this when he built his first park. Visitors were introduced to the cartoon drawings for the imaginative Disney, but when they went to Walt Disney Land, they were drawn there on the promise that this was a place where *Dreams Come True*. Others have opened and experienced success, but none have accomplished the distinctiveness known as Disney. Its ExtraOrdinary Competitive Advantage is retained today.

Retaining Your Competitive Advantage

Once you have gained an ExtraOrdinary Competitive Advantage in your respective field or at your dealership, you cannot live on your laurels forever. It requires constant monitoring and careful examination to stay at a superior position. Like Disney, Toyota and countless other companies you will need to employ strategies that keep your product or service on top.

The deployment of defensive strategies aimed at entrenching the advantage in the minds of customers can help. Defensive strategies are related to the offensive approaches of Cost Leadership and Differentiation, but while on defense you actually make it difficult for would-be competitors to make any headway or gain position.

The real keys to retaining your ExtraOrdinary Competitive Advantage through the deployment of defensive strategies are:

1) Innovation;
2) Technology;
3) Staff;
4) Service; and
5) Communication.

Innovation

Staying out front of new market entries and understanding how these developments could impact your product or service is essential to retaining your position. It is necessary to constantly look for new ways to improve your product or service and be willing to make critical adjustments. Resist the biggest deterrent to future success- today's success. Attend industry conferences, regularly read periodicals for the latest research and development ideas and conduct your own internal product testing to create new ways for improvement. Don't discount the value of customer complaints and input. The least expensive way to conduct research is to LISTEN to the ones who already pay you the favor of buying from you. Your competition is likely already doing these very things with your customer base. They are asking them questions about your product or service and looking for innovative ways they can reposition themselves in the marketplace by improving on what YOU do.

Technology

Faster than a speeding train is the rate at which technology is impacting your advantage. Actually, it is more like "light speed". So in order to retain your ExtraOrdinary Competitive Advantage, you will need to be quick to assess your position and ensure you are moving with and/or ahead of the next technological advancement. If you go to sleep in this area, when you wake up, you will have lost your spot.

Take for example the advancement of cell phone technology. It really was not that long ago that we were carrying cellphones around in a large bag strapped over our shoulders. A quantum leap was made from the traditional landline technology of many decades ago. However, once that technology gained ground as a viable alternative to the former, it took off like a rocket heading into outer space. In the last twenty-five years, we have essentially seen the eradication of the home phone and its replacement with mobile cell phones. No, not just cell phones, but smartphones. They come in a variety of shapes, sizes and colors but they are not all equal. IPhone, Android and Samsung are all terms we are familiar with today. Admittedly, we may not understand all we need to about the technology, but we know the companies who provide the best and who have gained the competitive advantage in the marketplace.

If your company provides a product, you need to be aware of the advancements in technology to retain your competitive advantage. There are fewer customers today with "flip phones" than those with "smartphones". These customers probably desire relatable technology in their computer programs. If your product runs on a legacy platform, you will find it difficult to hold on to your advantage without resorting to new defensive strategies. These type programs have been replaced by an Internet download and the local server to be replaced with an offsite server or the "Cloud" for data storage. The smartphone offers convenience and instant access. The same can be said about the move from compact disk data storage to flash drives. Most laptop computers built today do not have compact disk drives. To stay on top, you must constantly invest in new technological advancements.

Staff

Yvonne, from our first example in this chapter, is a prime example of what it takes to retain one's competitive advantage. Making sure you have the right people, with the right motivation, the right skills, and the right tools are paramount. It is not enough to have "sufficient" staff, you must have "the right" staff. Invest in them, train them, encourage them, pay them well, and help them help you be successful in creating a clear picture of your uniqueness, distinctive difference and advantage in the minds of your customers. Give them regular feedback on their performance. Empower them to do their job. Support their efforts to attain satisfied customers.

Service

Service can be a serious differentiation. When you can get your product to the consumer quicker without reducing its quality then customers may prefer you to the competition even if your product costs more. However, if your cost exceeds 15 to 20 percent over industry norms, then customers may have a hard time justifying the added cost. This factor of time and convenience is more prevalent with the millennial age buyers. More and more it seems the millennials are less satisfied to wait for things. They conduct research before purchasing and make many of their purchases online. It is particularly important to provide prompt, efficient service to this customer group, as they will often simply move on to another provider with little or no explanation to you. Also, packaging your product or service with added bonuses such as guarantees, training or technical support at no charge will also increase customer willingness to do business with you. The key is to consistently deliver on your service. Do more not less whenever possible. Expend time and energy to know your customer preferences and then when you provide service, make sure you exceed their expectations.

Communication

Maintaining a relationship with your customers creates an advantage that most companies today ignore or fail to capture. In addition to the communication at transaction time, it is increasingly apparent that customers today want to do business with companies that maintain a presence online via social media. Having a Google responsive website with mobile applications where potential and current customers can interact with you is vital. Utilizing a corporate Facebook account, Twitter, Periscope and/or YouTube is also helpful in communicating with your customers. But these are just tools. To distinguish yourself from the competition, you must do the things they are not doing in this area. Monthly newsletters (even for customers after the sale), promotional materials, catalogues (printed and online), and direct mail efforts to display new products or enhanced service are all ways to increase the lines of communication. Also, make it easy for your customers to talk to you when they need to discuss an issue. Long waits on the telephone are not an advantage, but a disadvantage. Rude customer service providers or technicians answering calls are killers. Call center staff trained to say "no" rather than to look for ways to help will for certain create a picture in the mind of your customer that will destroy the advantage you have worked so hard to attain. Always be looking for ways to talk with your customers.

The bottom line is this. To retain your ExtraOrdinary Competitive Advantage, you must continually provide something phenomenal. You cannot be satisfied with where you are today. It is imperative that you strive to provide something to your customers that your competition is unwilling or incapable of providing. And of course, it is critically important that your product or service remain relevant to the needs and wants of the customer.

In conclusion, the ExtraOrdinary Competitive Advantage is more than just keeping a leg up on the competition. Scott McKain, internationally known speaker and author says, "you must create distinction." In as many ways as possible, you and your team must strive to deliver to your customers a product or service so unusual, exemplary, astonishing, sensational, incredible or unbelievable that they choose you not only the first time, but every time! In your quest to gain and retain the ExtraOrdinary Competitive Advantage, focus the customer on the "Extra" about your product or service, not the "Ordinary" features or benefits.

BIO: MARTY COATES
Co-founder and President,
Waymaker Learning Corporation

Marty Coates is a trainer and consultant to independent automobile dealers across the country. He has trained more than 10,000 dealer participants in the past four years alone. He maintains a License Sales Representative card in North Carolina. His passion for helping dealers succeed drives him to travel more than 180 days a year on average.

He is President and Senior Consultant of Coates and Associates, Inc., a consulting, training and speaking firm he started in 1992. He has presented keynote speeches and conference training to groups in many foreign countries and all across the United States. Marty has led a number of companies during his twenty-six year career, to include serving as CEO of FirstChoice Healthcare, PC.

He is co-founder of Waymaker Learning Corporation. Marty produces and writes his online blog, "The Coates Perspective," where he discusses current business and social issues.

A graduate of North Carolina State University (NCSU), Marty has completed graduate level work in Business Administration at NCSU and Webster University. He has extensive leadership training from many military schools via his 15 plus year career as an officer in the United States Army, U.S. Army Reserves and Army National Guard. He is a decorated veteran of Operation Desert Storm where he was awarded a Bronze Star.

Marty is a co-author of two Amazon.com best-selling books namely, *Think and Grow Rich Today* and *Transform* (with Brian Tracy). He has authored or contributed to a number of other books to include, *The Waymaker Principles...Eight Keys to Living a Meaningful Life*, *Race to The Finish Line* and the national award-winning work entitled *Roadmap To Quality*.

Contact Information:
Marty Coates
Waymaker Learning Corporation

1082 Greenview Drive
Florence, South Carolina 29501

www.waymakerlearningcorp.com
843-229-3546

WAYMAKER
LEARNING
CORPORATION

CORPORATE TRAINING	CONSULTING	PUBLISHING
Strategic Planning	Business	Business
Management	Management	Self-Improvement
Organizational Development	Personnel	
Sales	Compliance	
Customer Service		
Marketing		

www.waymakerlearningcorp.com

843.229.3546

CHAPTER TWO

Gaining and Retaining The Competitive Advantage Across Multiple Platforms

By Jason Reaves

Since 1973, Wayne Reaves has been active in the business world. During this time, the world has changed dramatically, but the philosophy that has made our business successful has not changed. There is a core set of principles that we try to focus on every day so that we will continue to have success across all of our businesses. The small details of running a business can easily distract you, but if you want to truly succeed you must have the vision of where you want to be tomorrow. What do you want to accomplish, and how are you going to get there? There are five (5) Must Do's that you will have to keep at the top of your list and live by every day that you are in business. Are you willing to embrace change? How are you going to market your product or service so that it will be a success? Do you have a solid knowledge of your product? Are you willing to make a decision? Do you have the right employees in place?

Are you willing to embrace change?

To succeed in the business world as an entrepreneur, you have to understand that this world is constantly evolving, and you have to be ready to embrace changes in life, or as Wayne puts it "Turn over that new page in life." If you are not willing to be flexible and look on the horizon and see where the market is headed, you will be left behind holding onto an old product or service. In 1973, Wayne Reaves was working for a finance company in Macon, Georgia. Almost every day, he saw good people being turned down for credit as they tried to purchase a vehicle to get to work. It was at that time that he saw the need for a different kind of business, one that would finance bad credit customers and give them a second chance in life. The decision would be difficult. He would have to give up a weekly paycheck and take a big risk in life to fulfill his dream, but he was willing to make the sacrifice. His product was going to be simple. He was going to sell and finance a solid form of transportation to someone with bad credit so that they could get to work and provide for their family. It seems like such a simple concept today, but that is only because early Buy Here Pay Here lots took a chance with that model so many years ago. Are you willing to make a change in your life to become successful?

The advantage that he had over the competition was that he was able to approve the customer for a loan, not on their past credit history, but on the fact that they had a job, or a means to pay, and a desire to pay. In addition, since he was the one who bought and sold the car, it made the entire process that much easier. In a regular loan, the bank or finance company is providing the money, and the only chance they have to make a profit is through interest. The car lot sold the car, and the only chance they had to make a profit was through the original sale. Once the initial transaction took place, the sale was over and a little bit of profit was made. But in a Buy Here Pay Here operation, Wayne Reaves was able to make some money on the sale of the car as well as interest on the money that was part of the loan. By being able to make a profit on both sides of the transaction, the cost per sale went down tremendously. The same real estate that was used to sell the car was used to collect the money without additional rent. The same employees that were used to sell the car were also used to collect the money.

At this point in his life, he could have continued to operate his dealership and make a very comfortable living, but as an entrepreneur, he had the drive and work ethic and perhaps as important, the vision to search for new ideas for income. He was also able to embrace a change in life again when he sat down with state Representatives to author a new law in the state of Georgia. He wanted to start a business pawning car titles. While you could actually pawn a car, you would have had to keep the customer's car at your business until they redeemed the pawn ticket. While Wayne did have a large car lot, he had no intention of turning his car lot into a parking garage for pawned vehicles. He looked for another way to be able to get it done, and he convinced the state of Georgia to make it legal to pawn the title of the car instead of the car. He would have the first Title Pawn store in the state of Georgia.

Turning the page again, it had become obvious to Wayne that he needed something that didn't exist. He had been in the car business for around 14 years when he saw another opportunity that would become a business success story. By the late 1970s, his car lot had become so successful that he had to embrace a new type of technology. During tax season, his Buy Here Pay Here lot was delivering so many cars, that the ladies in the back office were unable to keep up with the amount of paperwork that was being generated. He needed a way to type in the customer's information, along with the vehicle information, and have something that would calculate the correct numbers and print all of the necessary paperwork. He invested money and time into his business by hiring a computer programmer who would write a very early and crude version of a modern day Dealer Management System, and he retained an attorney who would help him design legal forms to be used during the sales process that would help protect his dealership.

In the early 1980s, Wayne had become noticed by local leaders and had won the small business of the year by the City of Macon, GA, and become President of the local chapter of the Jaycees, a national civic organization that helps develop young business leaders. He had also been asked by the Governor of Georgia to teach education classes that would help keep the independent dealers out of trouble. He taught the first Pre-license and later, continuing education classes for used car dealers in the state of Georgia. As part of this process, he noticed that the used car dealers needed a system that could mimic what he had done at his car lot. The paperwork that they were producing was not correct, and many of them were unable to profit at their business because they could not keep up with the records and accounting. It was at this time that he decided to put on his first Buy Here Pay Here classes to teach other dealers how they could make more money and obey the laws on contracts, collections and repossessions. He rolled out the box, as many other dealers called it. It was a funny looking device with a keyboard and a printer that suddenly made their business life much easier. The Wayne Reaves Dealer Management System had been born, and change was coming to the Wayne Reaves businesses again.

Even with his car and other businesses alive and booming, Wayne Reaves was ready to step out of his comfort zone again and begin the process of building another business one customer at a time. There were many challenges to this change. Most dealerships had never heard of a computer system, much less seen one. How were they going to be trained, and what forms were they going to use to help their dealership stay in compliance? The only way to make this work would be to leave behind the days of pounding the pavement at the car lot and hit the road with seminars to teach dealerships the correct way to run a buy here pay here business. He would provide the knowledge, hardware, software, and forms that a dealership needed to run their operation. It would be a one stop shop for the car dealership.

In the early days, he would drive to dealerships throughout the Southeast to train, sell and install software, as well as, lead training classes that would attract dealers from all over the country wanting the knowledge that he had attained in the car business. He would soon need to make another change that would propel him to another level. Time is valuable, and we were limited by travel time as the company's customer base reached further into the Southeast. Wayne decided it was time to purchase an airplane and hire a full time pilot. This would allow him to double the number of dealerships that he could meet with in a given day. He would load the airplane full of computers, fly into airports where the dealerships would pick him up and take him to their office for training. Until the internet became wide spread, this was the only way to grow the business.

This all led to another big change. The growth of the internet allowed us to help dealers install and run their programs without leaving the comfort of our offices, thereby increasing our sales potential and lowering costs. It was time to pass some of these savings along to the customer. Anytime you have a change in a price for your product, whether it is up or down, danger could be around the corner. How are customers going to respond? If the price goes up, will they continue to buy? If the price goes down, will enough people buy the product to keep the company in business? It would be a risky move, but Wayne Reaves was up for the challenge. Wayne calculated and crunched numbers and over a period of several years in the early 2000's the software shifted from a license purchase with a monthly support fee to a true Software as a Service model. As this was occurring, we were developing and moving forward with what he truly believed was the future and another big change to the way we conducted business. While, he believed that the new pricing structure would grow the business there was a "new wrinkle" as Wayne would call it on the horizon. He was going to embrace new programming that would continue to secure his place as a leader in the dealer management software industry.

By looking into the future, seeing where the market was headed, and making a decision based on the customer's satisfaction level, Wayne Reaves was able to determine that if we hired a national law firm to design compliant PDF's, or plain paper forms as they were called, the dealership would benefit tremendously. No longer would the dealership have to worry about lining up a form in a dot matrix printer or worse, running out of forms on a busy sales day and not being able to sell any more cars. It would be a risky change for the income model that we had utilized for many years. The sale of forms would all but be over, and in its place would be the unknown. We were willing to embrace that change, and in return, we experienced a large growth in the company. It had worked!

In addition to all of these changes, it was time for another change in the development world. Sometimes you have to embrace change that is not based on additional revenue, but on continuing to be a leader in the market. When Wayne first started in the software business, the program ran and stored the data on something called 5 ¼" floppy drives. In fact, high end computers had two of these drives so that you did not have to swap them out! We watched the computer world grow the days of the 286, 386, 486, and finally, the Pentium processor. When Microsoft released a new operating system called Windows 95, it was time for a change. The software that had taken years to develop over multiple platforms had to be re-worked from the ground up in a new Windows environment. This meant that new installations on windows machines would require dealers to have to learn how to use a mouse. A lot of money was spent on programming to get our DOS system users to embrace the Windows program. Wayne was insistent that our highly skilled programmers spend extra time programming in order that the transition to a windows environment would not be an issue for our average user.

Microsoft didn't stop there, however, and neither did the Internet. It was time to invest even more money into an even bigger overhaul. While Windows programs are still a viable option today, the future is on the web and the Wayne Reaves Company saw it coming and invested millions into a product that would run over the internet. This is an example of where Wayne and his company look into the future and stepped out even though the need was not yet widespread. The new, modern and sometimes even mobile dealerships no longer have to worry about server and networking expenses. They can run multiple stores from any of their locations. In fact, thanks to the online movement, they can access their data from anywhere in the world. Wayne Reaves is not done yet; we have already looked into the future and are working on the latest technology changes to make sure that our customers are always running the best product.

There would still be many more changes to come for dealerships with the explosion of the Internet and advertising was among the first. With the knowledge of how advertising had changed our lives in 1975, it was time to get behind the marketing side of the car business and make the Wayne Reaves Company a complete solution for the car dealership. We were going to provide an inexpensive but highly effective marketing tool to the dealerships that would be completely integrated with the Dealer Management Software. New inventory and pictures would automatically appear on their website, and leads would be downloaded directly into Wayne Reaves Dealer Management software. No one else in our marketplace had combined these two items before, and it was a gamble that was going to pay off. (On a side note, within two years of the release of this new product, the crash of 2008 hit. Dealerships began closing their doors at an incredible rate as the sale of vehicles plummeted, but Wayne Reaves continued to grow during this period, and looking back, we are very proud to say that we never had to lay anyone off during that time.) This process would coincide with the movement to Electronic Temp Tags and Title Registration that Wayne Reaves would be heavily involved in beginning in Florida, then Georgia, and with the Carolinas moving into that direction at the time of the publishing of this book.

The world is always changing, and you must find a way to adapt to these changes and look for new growth potential. We are currently releasing the next generation of our dealer websites that will not only be mobile first, but will also use single page application technology. We will continue to invest in products and look forward to the next exciting challenges.

How are you going to Market your product?

Now that we have talked about embracing change, let's talk about the next key to gaining a competitive advantage- Marketing. What good would the next big idea be if no one knew about it? In advertising, you have to have product awareness and you have to have branding.

If we go back to the early car lot days for Wayne Reaves, he was able to sell some cars every month, but his market was limited to friends and family of existing customers and ride by traffic that happened to stop in. If that sounds familiar, it would be the 1970's version of Facebook. He could have stayed a small car lot, but that was not in his plans. Wayne wanted to have the biggest Buy Here Pay Here operation in middle Georgia. He did not want to be the little guy on the corner, and he knew the only way to get there would be to spread the word of his products to more people. He took two bold moves that would change his hold on the Buy Here Pay Here market in middle Georgia for the next 27 years.

Although it is not true for all businesses, for example, the software business, location is a very critical part of marketing when deciding where to put your business. You are not going to sell a new BMW in a blue collar part of town and you are not going to sell a Buy Here Pay Here car in the best part of town. He moved his car lot from downtown Macon, as other businesses were also leaving due to the new mall that was being built on the edge of town, to one of the busiest streets in Macon. It wasn't just any busy street, but the street that took blue collar Macon from the neighborhoods that they lived in to the places where they worked- Highway 247 or Pio Nono Avenue. Traffic would back up for miles in the morning and afternoon allowing customers to drive very slowly in front of the cars lined up with big letters that read Buy Here Pay Here scribbled across the front of the windshield. Streamers hung from the light poles, and the smell of free grilled hot dogs carried across the street to one of the malls. Wayne Reaves had a philosophy. If he could get more people on the lot, he knew that he could sell more cars. Hot dogs and live radio broadcasts were just part of the marketing magic that would bring more people to the car lot on any given Saturday. To get even more attention, he had an electronic sign installed that would flash different messages across the screen to attract the customers. It would be the first in the middle Georgia area, and it was filled with standard clear light bulbs that would light up and go out to display scrolling and flashing words to grab potential customers' attention. While it did not compare to the full color LED boards of today, it was an attention grabber in the 1980s to say the least. In fact, one of the more common requests would be from local politicians during election times.

Finally, to cap off the bold move, he launched a television campaign in a time when only the franchise stores advertised. He knew that he had a limited budget, and he needed to get the most bang for his buck. He needed a television commercial that people would remember. He wanted people to know that Wayne

Reaves (The Real Wayne) was the "Walking Man's Friend." He came up with a series of commercials that were legendary and are still remembered by people in middle Georgia today, and it worked. His small operation became one of the largest Buy Here Pay Here Stores in middle Georgia for years to come. Advertising works; do not overlook it in your business.

Years later, as Wayne Reaves moved into the software business, advertising would prove much more of a challenge, but in order to be successful and stay ahead of any competition, it had to be done. There were over 4000 independent dealers in Georgia alone. How could he get out and advertise this new software product to all of these dealers? The campaign started with direct mail and hundreds of phone calls made by a single employee in the office, but how were you going to advertise a software program when many people still didn't understand how a computer fit into their lives? He combined it with the education. The dealerships knew that they wanted to make money, and they wanted to stay out of trouble. This was the hot button. Dealerships came from all over the Southeast to learn how to get into and succeed in the Buy Here Pay Here business. Who would be a better person to learn from than someone who had actually been in the car business and succeeded for the last 14 years? He had taken a $5000 loan and a vision and turned it into an operation that would average close to 100 cars per month. They soon learned that they could not be successful without this new software program. They had to have it.

Do you have a solid knowledge of your product?

While that sounds simple enough, transitioning from someone who knows how to buy and sell cars to running a successful dealership is a major jump. Wayne Reaves knew how to buy cars. He knew how to sell cars and collect money. He had come out of the finance business where they had taught him everything he would ever need to know about collections. What else was there to know? After being in the car business for just a few years with everything seemingly going fine, Wayne was introduced to another profession that was really interested in the car business- the legal profession. He soon learned that bad paperwork meant bad deals. This was a life lesson. If you are going to be in business for yourself, you had better know the regulations and rules that involve your business or an attorney will teach them to you, and you will not be in business for very long.

Regulation Z, the used car board for Georgia, and the Federal Trade Commission are just a few of the regulatory agencies that were involved in the car business back in 1973. I believe that the used car dealer is one of the most regulated small businesses in this country. You need to know the agencies that are regulating you. Wayne Reaves spent years learning the car business inside and out, and it served him well while in the car business, and in the later years, the software business. You, too, will have to know the federal and state laws that affect your business. Do your homework and become well read in your business field.

These same laws that he had spent so much time learning as a car dealer would put him above the competition in the next stage of life. He had not only lived the car business and learned all of the regulations; he was now teaching these laws and regulations for the state. Years of experience serving in the role as an educator for the state helped to prepare him for the software business. A programmer would not know which repossession letter to use, that there was a maximum interest rate, or any of the hundreds of compliance issues that come up every day in the car business. He would have to teach these laws to the programmers and other key employees in the software business. One of the biggest lessons that he taught me in the business world is that laws and regulations are constantly changing. You are never through learning in life. In your business, you need to have multiple sources for information, whether it is state and industry associations, legal subscriptions or business publications. As a company, we attend over 30 national and state meetings each year. We subscribe to multiple legal services that help keep us abreast of coming changes, and there are three people in the company who teach Continuing Education Classes. While it is impossible to know everything about your business, if you want to be successful, you have to learn everything you can.

There is another side to knowing your business. You need to know your competition. First, just because they sell the same product as you does not mean that they are your competition. Both Starbucks and McDonalds sell coffee, but I would never place them as competition for each other. If you are McDonalds, you need to worry about Burger King, and if you are Starbucks, you need to worry about the small gourmet coffee stores. There may be a car dealership down the street from your location, but it does not mean that they are in direct competition with you. Sure, you are both selling cars, but are you catering to the same customer base? You certainly need to keep an eye on all businesses that sell the same product that you are selling, but you need to study the direct competition. What are they selling? How are they selling it? What price are they selling it for? How can I make a better product, and finally, are they making money? The first four questions do not really matter in the long term if they are not making money, and we are all in business to make money.

Make a decision today

Wayne Reaves has always described himself as an action person no matter what business he was running. If your sales approach is not working, change it today. If an employee is not doing their job, hire someone else today. I could write 100 pages of examples on this subject, but the most important lesson is do not procrastinate. Trust your instinct; it is what got you here in the first place. If a procedure is not working in your office, do not delay. It does not mean that you have to make a decision in the next five minutes, but it does mean that you need to put all of your effort into figuring out how you need to change it, and once you have decided on a direction, do not wait. Start the implementation of it today. Many decisions may take months or years to implement, but if you do not get started, the final implementation will just take that much longer, or you will never get started at all.

Just because you make a decision today, does not mean that you cannot change your mind. Wayne has always told me that "You are not perfect. Everyone will make mistakes, but if you do nothing, you will have regret." If you make a change, the worst thing that can happen is that the change did not fix the problem, but at least you can say that you tried. You stayed in the fight. If the Chevrolet is not selling, go buy some Fords. If the customer cannot afford $1,500 down, lower the down payment. If a salesman cannot sell, go hire someone else. Don't turn your business into a government bureaucracy. Make a decision today.

Hire the Right Employees

Key employees are one of the most important parts of any business. They can truly make or break your business with the decisions that they make and the service that they give your customer. As a child, I very distinctly remember the employees Wayne viewed as the best collectors, sales people, mechanics and office personnel for one reason. He talked about them like they were friends and family at the dinner table, and he spent time with them outside of the work place so that they could get to know each other. They well understood his philosophy in business, the rules that they needed to follow, and the service that they were to give to the customer. They were aware of the decisions that they could make, as well as, the gray area where they needed to ask the boss. They were not a key employee when they were hired, but he would quickly decide if he was able to work with them day to day, and then, he would train them to become a key employee.

One of the biggest differences between being in the car business and being in the software business is the available pool of employees and the length of time it takes to train them. As mentioned earlier, Wayne had to train the programmers to think like car dealers. We also have to train our sales people and the customer service representatives to understand the car business, as well as, the software business. When an employee is unable to do their job, you have to ask yourself if the employee failed to learn or did you fail to train. We have always tried to make sure that some of our employees are very technical and some really understand the car business, but in the end, we make sure that both are provided years of training opportunities.

As one final note, if you want to have these key employees, training is never over. Remember earlier when we talked about keeping informed about your business, as well as, the competition? If you have done your research and kept abreast of the changes, you have only done half of your job. The other half of your job is to make sure that your employees have that same knowledge.

Closing

It takes hard work and dedication to open and run multiple businesses, but I believe that we have navigated the daily challenges in the business world by continuing to follow the principles that my Dad instilled in me from a very young age. We continue to embrace change, market our products, study our business, make quick decisions, and hire the right people to help us do it all. We wish you the best of luck in your business.

BIO: JASON REAVES
President at Wayne Reaves Software

Jason began his automotive career with the highly successful Wayne's Auto Sales, a Buy Here Pay Here Lot in Macon, Ga . His family opened their lot in 1973 when Jason was a young boy and he became familiar with washing cars and all the hard work and long hours that it took to make the car lot the success it was!

In 1987 Wayne Reaves Software had launched. The family now had a new automotive business that was operated by the family alongside the car lot.

With a degree in Accounting from Mercer University, Jason was well placed to take on a major role in the software company where he presides today.

Jason is an outstanding leader and educator, he holds a position as one of the few licensed instructors for the state of Georgia pre license and continuing education required classes for auto dealers.

He sits on the board of the GIADA and communicates daily with industry leaders from consultants, to CPA's to attorneys. As a provider of software and forms that help dealers in more than 20 states stay compliant with state and federal laws, Jason has become one of the foremost authorities in the industry today.

With a staff of about 40 under his wing, he is always looking for solutions to help dealers be successful, because he and his staff know that the dealer must be in a position to succeed before his company ever can.

Contact Information:
Jason Reaves
Wayne Reaves Software
(800) 701-8082
jason@waynereaves.com

CHAPTER THREE
Selling Through Psychology
By Jonathan Dawson

If you like psychology, you'll love this chapter! I believe that a salesperson or manager who understands why something works is more empowered, educated and effective. So, my goal is to share with you the principles that underline and support all the greatest sales techniques, some of which your people may already be using. A decade ago, I coined the word "Sellchology," which means understanding how to sell through psychology. This includes knowing what, how, and most importantly, WHY you should say or do something while with your customer.

In this chapter, I will share with you 7 principles of psychology that are currently influencing every customer interaction at your dealership. Every successful sales technique that has ever been used and every profitable process you have is based on these psychological principles:

1. **Proactivity** - Being proactive means that you anticipate and address the questions, concerns or challenges of your customer before they come up.
2. **Preparedness** - All top performing salespeople are prepared. Being prepared is the ability to anticipate and address questions, concerns or challenges when they come up.
3. **Pattern interrupt** - Interrupting someone's pattern of thought by doing or saying something they were not expecting in order to introduce a new idea or emotion to the customer.
4. **Give-Get** - The act of requiring that the customer give you something of value in return for getting something of value from you.

5. **Leverage** - Applying pressure using something the customer values in order to cause flexibility in another desired area.
6. **Influence** - There are 8 primary influencers of buying motives and buying behavior: Scarcity, Contrast, Commitment, Authority, Social Proof, Exemption, Familiarity, and Obligation.
7. **Value** - I believe there are 6 core values that customers have. They are Freedom, Time, Money, Identity, Security, and Space. When the value you add exceeds the price you are asking, people buy. Therefore, mastering the ability to add value is critical to sales success.

All seven of these principles provide the building blocks for a successful process, word track, or approach to selling and serving more customers in the most customer-centric way possible. And because they are based on psychology, these principles will work on all of your customers.

Most sales books are filled with vague ideas but don't actually teach you how to implement them, but this book is different!

Let's begin with the idea of proactivity. Proactivity is defined as the ability to anticipate and address the questions and concerns of your customer <u>before</u> they come up. This is contrary to the commonly trained approach of "overcoming" objections, which is a more reactive model.

Imagine you are having dinner in a restaurant. Would you prefer that your server offer refills before you need them? Or would you prefer to flag your waiter down every time you need a refill on your drink? Most people find that the first (proactive) approach by a server creates a more enjoyable dining experience. Anticipatory service is by definition providing service prior to or in advance of a request. The anticipatory server would proactively offer to satisfy a common request or concern before a request has been made. I believe salespeople should adopt the same approach and proactively address common questions, concerns or objections during the sales process. Just as every server should know that a restaurant customer needs menus, silverware, and refills, car salespeople should know that customers will ask about price, payments, or trade-in values. Proactive selling through anticipatory service will completely transform the customer experience.

I call it becoming a PRO. The first step to becoming a PRO-active salesperson is making a list of the most common questions, issues, concerns, or objections that you experience in a typical conversation with a customer. From the greeting to the close, there are probably 10 to 20 common questions or concerns that show up all the time. Learn to offer solutions to these issues and introduce objections so that you don't have to overcome them later. Similar to being offered a refill prior to requesting one, when concerns are brought up proactively, they are received in a completely different perspective and will positively change the dynamic of your customer interaction.

To begin implementing proactive selling, start by making a list of what is common. For example, in the greeting, the typical customer says the following things: *"just looking","* *not buying today"*, *"you're my first stop"*, *"I don't have much time"*, *"I just want your best price"*, and so on. When you're done with the list, the next step is to create word tracks or approaches that introduce the objections or concerns proactively. By reframing and rephrasing the questions or concerns in a more positive tone you will introduce the objection first, so you do not need to overcome it.

Let's look at some examples. Instead of waiting for a customer to say, *"I'm just looking"* consider greeting them with, *"Welcome, are you folks doing some looking and shopping today?"* This proactive approach eliminates the ability of the customer to use "just looking" against you. Take the common issue of *"I don't have much time"* and proactively rephrase it into, *"I know your time is valuable"* prior to them mentioning time constraints. Or, before a customer would say, *"You are my first stop,"* introduce the idea first by asking them, *"Do we get to be your first stop or have you been to a few places already?"* Just like in the refill example, by raising the topic first (proactively anticipating), the concern is reframed in a much more friendly and customer service oriented tone.

Here is an example of using proactive selling during the number's presentation phase. If you can tell your customer is reluctant, why wait until she tells you, *"I want to think about it?"* Instead, consider suggesting to her, *"Let's take a minute to recap what we've talked about so far to see what you think."* Then recap the situation together. After all, I would much rather offer for them to take time to think while they are with me than wait until they tell me they are going to go home and think about it. My version of thinking about it includes me; their version does not.

My experience using this proactive approach and my students nationwide have proven that virtually all sales situations are better handled in an anticipatory and proactive manner. Every objection you struggle with can be eliminated if you find a positive way to bring it up first.

What if the salesperson gets asked a question before they can be proactive? That's a great question…

Being prepared means having a plan for what to do when objections do come up. Salespeople are often stumped by some of the most common questions: price, trade, payments, rates or availability.

What do salespeople normally do when these things come up? Let's say the customer asks, *"What's the best price you can do on this car?"* Most salespeople typically pass the buck and say, *"That's not my job. I'm not the one who handles that. Have you driven it yet?"* If customers ask about payments, salespeople usually sound like this, *"I'm not the one who will calculate the final payments. My finance manager does that. My job is to find you the right car. Do you know what you'd like to look at?"* Deflect and redirect is what usually happens. I do not think this approach is customer-oriented and would like to propose a new and better way.

I developed a simple 6-step process that will make a lot of sense once you learn it. You can remember the steps by using the acronym "T.H.A.N.K.S." Each step starts with a letter from this word:

> **Thank** – Thank them for asking the question
> **Help** – Let them know you can Help
> **Address** - Address their question by sharing the factors involved
> **Need** – Share with them that you Need more information from them
> **Keep** – Keep asking questions to clarify
> **Summarize** – Do a Summary of what you're going to do for them

Let's start with the 1st letter. T stands for "Thank the customer." When a customer asks you a question about anything including price, trade, payments, rates or availability, your first response should be to thank them. It may sound like this, *"Thanks for asking. I appreciate this question."*

H is for Help. You might say something like, *"I can Help you with that."* You want to let the customer know they're talking to the right person so you may say, *"I am the right person to answer that for you."*

A stands for Address. In step 3, address the question the customer asked. The basic idea is simply to say: *"There are several factors I need to address in order to help you..."* And then simply list the factors that may determine your answer to their question.

N stands for Need. You will let the customer know that you need more information in order to answer their question. It sounds like this, *"I need to ask you just a couple of questions if that's okay."*

K stands for Keep. Keep asking questions! This step is really just about asking the customer a few questions. Make sure your questions are relevant to what the customer asked. So if they asked about trade, your questions need to be related to trade. If they asked about payments, your follow-up questions need to be related to payments.

The final step is S and it stands for Summarize. The goal of this step is to get the customer back on track with you, and back on the road to the sale. This step requires summarizing two things: the customer's original question and helping them get the new vehicle that they're shopping for. If they had asked about a payment this step may sound something like this, *"I hear you asking for 2 things: the payment (or price/trade/rate/whatever they asked about) is obviously important to you. And you want to get a vehicle that fits your needs. It sounds like you really need both in order to move forward. And if I can get you both, I probably have a good chance of doing business with you. Is that right?"*

Let's look at an example. If the customer asked a question about payments, the complete response would be, *"Thank you for asking. I can help you with that. There are some factors that will*

influence payments, such as rate, total amount financed, term, and if you want any extras in your loan. I need to ask some questions if that's okay. (Ask a few related questions). *It sounds like you're asking for 2 things: Payments that fit your budget are very important to you. And you need to find a new vehicle that fits your needs. If I can get you both, do I have a chance at your business?"*

If you practice these steps and learn to incorporate the T.H.A.N.K.S. technique in your presentation, you will find that most customers will respond positively as compared to how they might respond to the classic deflect and redirect method.

I have pudding in my pants but that's not what this section is about…

I use the pattern interrupt principle a lot in my training. Pattern interrupt is one of the most phenomenal techniques in psychology. It's interrupting someone's pattern of thought by doing or saying something they were not expecting in order to introduce a new idea or emotion. I have a fun story illustrating pattern interrupt. It is the best use of pattern interrupt I've ever personally experienced.

I was in my house relaxing on a Sunday, when I heard a knock on my door. I opened the door to find a smiling young man. The following conversation ensued:

Young man with a smile says, *"Good afternoon, sir. I have pudding in my pants. But that's not the reason I'm here."*
　　Me, confused, *"I'm sorry, you have what?"*
Young man still smiling, *"I have pudding in my pants, but that's not the reason I'm here and I'd rather not talk about it if that's okay with you."*
　　Me, really confused, *"What are you doing then? I don't understand."*

Young man with a bigger smile, *"Thanks for asking. And since you did, I'll tell you."*

He then reached in his back pocket and grabbed a brochure. He was offering magazine subscriptions. As he began to go through his presentation on the magazines, I was still confused about the whole pudding thing, but I saw where he was going. I said, *"Oh, okay, you're selling magazine subscriptions."*
Him, sounding confused, *"Actually, sir, the last thing I'm going to do is ask you to buy magazines today."*
Me, apologetic, *"I'm sorry, what are you doing then?"*
Him confident, *"Well, since you asked, I'll continue."*
He went right back into his presentation and a couple minutes later offered me a subscription and said, *"Based on what you told me, sir, I recommend this one and this one."*
I was now beyond confused, *"I thought you said you weren't going to try to sell me a magazine?"*
He replied without hesitation, *"Actually, sir, if you recall what I said was that the last thing I was going to do is sell you a magazine and this is the last thing. We're pretty much done here."*
At this point, I was hooked. He'd knocked me off my game so many times, I couldn't stand on my own two feet and he sold me three magazine subscriptions!

That was an example of a pattern interrupt. Great salespeople understand this principle and use it daily with their customers to keep the customer on their track instead of the customer's track. If at any point in the sale process you don't like the direction (pattern) of the sale, use a pattern interrupt to reset the conversation and direction. Important places to intentionally use the pattern interrupt are:
1. Greeting
2. Transitioning inside the store
3. Getting the demo drive
4. Coming in to look at numbers

5. Presenting the numbers for the first pencil
6. Manager early intervention (T.O.)
7. Closing
8. Asking for referrals

At any of these stages, the salesperson can struggle to transition to the next step. An appropriately executed pattern interrupt will dramatically change the perception and effectiveness of the next step to which you are moving.

Take presenting the numbers as an example. Humor can be a great pattern interrupt. With a smile try saying this, *"My therapist says I'm supposed to try and avoid stress and rejection as much as possible, so please limit your "no's" to no more than 2 please."* Or when asking for referrals use a pattern interrupt before asking, like this, *"Two things have happened today, one is good and one is not so good. The good news is that you're my customer and I'm happy for you. The not so good news is that I just lost my best prospect because you became a customer. So now there is a "best prospect" void that needs to be filled and since you created the problem by buying, you need to help me fill the void."*

All top performing sales professionals use some form of pattern interrupts to direct the attention and emotion of their customer. Your team should, too!

If you would like to get a FREE sample audio of some of the best pattern interrupt ideas I will be happy to give that to you, under one condition. Please send me an email with the subject line "pattern interrupt" to info@sellchology.com

The principle of give-get is the act of requiring the customer to GIVE you something of value in return for them GETting something of value. To incorporate this principle, ask your customer to give you something in return when they ask for something from you.

I think too often salespeople give-in instead of give-get whenever the customer asks for things, such as getting a lower payment or more for their trade. I encourage you to start using the principle of give-get. In fact, there is a phrase you should learn and use. This phrase is extremely powerful because it's based in psychology: *"I am happy to do that for you - under one condition."* When you say this phrase, it's a type of pattern interrupt because the customer doesn't expect this to happen. Then you can introduce your condition. Your conditions could be putting more cash down, or considering a different color, or getting a co-signer. The idea is you need to ask for something in return. Otherwise, you're conditioning customers to simply get rewarded for asking for things.

Some of my students use the principle of give-get to get more referrals. The next time a customer wants a discount, turn the tables by saying, *"I'm excited. You and I are about to come to agreement on this deal. I can feel it. We're close. You're looking for an extra $500. I'm willing to look into that under one condition. Don't send me to my manager empty-handed."* Then place a sheet of paper in front of them with 10 blanks and say, *"I need ten names and ten numbers of ten people that I can call on after I sell you this truck. That way when I go to management, I'll have something that shows you're serious about doing business."*

Start applying the principle of give-get by saying, *"I'm happy to do this for you – under one condition."*

Your team struggles with some of these simple strategies because they don't know them or how to do them and it costs you sales and profit, but you don't need to keep struggling, you can and should help them learn these strategies and principles. When your people fail, you fail!

Another powerful principle in psychology is leverage. Leverage is applying pressure using something of value in order to cause movement in another desired area. There's nothing wrong with pressuring someone to buy IF you're using the right pressure for the right reasons. I believe that if you care about people, you should pressure them to do the right thing for themselves. If my friend were thinking of leaving his family, I would pressure him to stay and fight for his family. And I pressure my customers to do business with me if I believe it's the right thing for them. But again, you need to use it the right way for the right reasons.

Understanding leverage means you find out what the core leverage is that you have with a customer to get them to take action. Here is an example. I was in Iowa working with a dealership sales team, and this salesperson was trying to close a deal with a couple on a van. I had observed the husband for a couple hours and noticed that he'd gone through several cigarettes. Early in the process I had casually asked this customer if he normally smoked this much. He said, no, not normally. He also told me that he wants to quit and has been trying to quit for years because he doesn't want his kids to start smoking when they get older.

When I went in on the close, I knew that this gentleman wanted to buy the van, but the monthly payment was $60 higher than he originally wanted. As a close, I said, *"Folks, I know the payment is higher than you want for your monthly budget. I also know, Sir, that you want to quit smoking, and that right now you're smoking enough cigarettes a month to offset this payment. So the real question is, do you want your wife and kids to get this new van or do you want to keep a habit that you know is hurting you? I'll let you guys talk about it and I'll go ahead and get the van cleaned for delivery."* As I was walking away, I could see on his face he knew he was stuck. I had leverage.

Your team needs to learn how to use leverage the right way and for the right reasons. Everyone who has ever bought a vehicle has decided to exchange their money for something they wanted more than their money. And the reason they did it was leverage.

You'll either do these strategies because you've seen others trying to change and you want to change, too, or because you feel obligated to your people since they put in so much time. Or perhaps you'll try them because you like the ideas and they resonate with you. Whatever the reasons are, they are your reasons...

There are eight major influencers of buying behavior. They were described by Dr. Robert Cialdini in his book *Influence: The Psychology of Persuasion*. I'll show how to apply these principles in the sale process at your dealership.

The first influencer is social proof. It means using group or culture to influence an individual. When you use social proof to influence someone, you use the idea of 'everybody else is doing this so it's safe for you to do it, too.' Simple ways to implement social proof is intentionally using reviews, video testimonials, and photos of happy customers to help future customers feel safe about buying from you.

One of my favorite principles is obligation/reciprocity. The idea behind it is using a sense of indebtedness to cause someone to take action. The more value potential customers perceive or receive from you, the more obligation to reciprocate (buy from you) they feel. Value can be added in many simple ways. See the next section (6 core values) in this chapter to learn how to add value.

The next principle is liking and familiarity. People are influenced by people that they feel are similar to them or that they're familiar with. You're more likely to influence somebody if he or she can relate to you. Also, if a customer feels that a salesperson genuinely likes them, they will want to do more for them. To use this influencer, look for common things you have with your customer. Also, find something you like about them and genuinely compliment them on it.

The next core influencer of behavior is commitment and consistency. Commitments and promises are very important to some people. They feel they need to do what they said they were going to do. Using trial closes with this group of customers is a great way to utilize this principle. Also, it is critical for you to keep your promises and commitments to influence them.

The principle of higher authority is a powerful influencer. It's the idea that an expert in an area will influence others because he or she is perceived to have special knowledge or power. The goal of your sales team should be to do and say things that elevate their perceived authority.

Scarcity is principle # 6. The principle of scarcity is using the fear of loss, or the desire to have a limited model, or the desire to have access to something of value that's not readily available. There are some people who will buy simply because this is the last model or because special programs are about to end. Scarcity drives behavior and influences some of your buyers.

The contrast principle is #7 on the list of influencers. The contrast principle involves comparing two things back to back. If the first request is considerably larger, and the second request is smaller, the second request is more likely to be received because of the immediate contrast. For example, if you ask a customer for 30 referrals first, then say you'll settle for 10, you are likely to get 10. The first request of 30 was so big that 10 seems reasonable in contrast.

The last principle is the exemption principle. The exemption principle is the opposite of scarcity. It's a type of reverse psychology because some people believe they're the exception to the rule. So, if you tell these people a program will end, their response is, *"No, it won't; it will probably get extended."* Knowing this, you simply practice reverse requests on them, such as letting them know the chances are that the program will get extended. This will compel them to say, *"Well, you don't know that it'll get extended."* To which you respond, *"You're right - it's better to not risk it since you already know this is the right car and you want it. Let's do it now."*

If you think about these 8 principles and your customers, you've probably realized that different things influence different people. You have to identify which influencer is the best for everyone. Remember, it's always easier to influence someone when you know what already influences him or her.

I know your time is valuable and you have many other choices of things to do instead of reading this chapter. I hope that you get a ton of value from this section and I am confident that this information will transform your customer experience!

Many salespeople struggle with the idea of adding value. Adding value is not the same as offering discounts. I'll share the six values that I believe everyone has and how to add each one in your sales process.

Here are the six core values of your customers:
1. Freedom
2. Time
3. Money
4. Identity
5. Security
6. Space

How do you add these values? Let's start with the value of freedom. In a sales context, freedom has to do with having choices and options. Customers want to feel free and not be constrained in any way. To add value of freedom, talk in terms of options, freedom, and choice. Here is an example. After greeting a customer on the lot, consider saying something like this, *"Thanks for visiting our dealership. As you can see, we have* **hundreds of vehicles**. *And based on what you've told me, I think we have at least* **100 options** *that would fit your situation. And speaking of* **options**, *I know that where you buy a car is* **your choice** *and I appreciate you giving us a chance to be the better* **choice**.*"* The idea here is to find ways to talk in terms of options, flexibility, freedom, and choices whenever possible.

Your customers also value their time because it's such a limited resource. To add the value of time, your goal should be to speak and act in a way that shows you value their time. This includes saying things like, *"I know your time is valuable"*, *"I want to be respectful of your time"* or *"What would you like to accomplish with the time that you have today?"* You can also do simple things like moving with urgency - put some pep in your step, put some slide in your glide! Move with intentionality and purpose to show the customer that you value their time.

In general, most customers also value their money. To add the value of money, talk about savings, discounts, and special incentives - language like that tells the customer that you understand that they value their hard-earned money. Remember, however, that at some point, everybody values something more than they value their money. And as soon as they value a vehicle more than money, they give up their money for that vehicle.

The next core value of your customers is identity. Most people value their identity and personal information. This is why it can be hard to get people to open up about simple things like where they work, or to share their email and phone number. As an example, add the following language to your greeting and presentation: *"I'd like to find out what you're trying to accomplish and a little bit about you, so that I can better understand how to help you today"* or *"I'm not going to ask you a bunch of financial questions and credit questions up front. That's none of my business yet."*

Let's discuss the value of security next. Security is not just the physical safety of the car and the physical environment for your customers. The value of security is also your customer's emotional safety and their fear of making a mistake in the transaction. As you well know, some people come to the lot feeling apprehensive and may be afraid of making a mistake by choosing the wrong car or dealership. To help a customer feel a sense of emotional security, I encourage you to start using language such as, *"excellent choice"*, and *"you're doing the right thing"*. When you use language like that, the customer starts to feel a sense of emotional security in the transaction. Also, when you say things such as *"I'm confident"* and *"I'm the right person to help you,"* you also increase their security by increasing your higher authority.

The last value is space. People value their personal space and also want to feel comfortable in the environment they're in. To add the value of space, consider using a different greeting where you don't shake hands every time. Most salespeople start in the "public space," go through a person's "social space," right into a customer's "personal space" to shake someone's hand. The reason many customers respond negatively to this approach and give weak handshakes is because you've violated their value of space. The best way to get the customer to give you what they value is by giving them values of freedom, time, money, identity, security and space first.

You've just learned some of the most important principles of psychology. You may have known some already, but others may have been eye-opening. When racing to the finish line, remember that the race is filled with people. This is a people business so psychology is always influencing your sales. I hope this chapter will help you win the race by helping you sell through psychology!

BIO: JONATHAN W. DAWSON
Car Salesman | Trainer | Speaker
Consultant | Coach | Author

Ask Jonathan Dawson what his mission is and you will always get the same answer, "I want to save the world, one salesperson at a time." His passions are: teaching truths that TRANSFORM, coaching that creates CHANGE, and influencing that leaves an IMPACT.

Jonathan is known for his conversational teaching style and common sense approach. Whether he is speaking at a national automotive conferences or writing articles for automotive blogs and magazines, he keeps his information fresh because he is in dealerships every month and he still sells cars. Having been in thousands of dealerships in over a decade across the country, his goal is to help dealerships learn how to "out-experience" their competition by creating a truly unique culture.

His company, LITE Consulting, Inc. provides dealership employees with Sellchology - "Selling through Psychology." This approach is a combination of customer-focused selling, community-driven marketing, and impact-focused leadership

Contact Information:

Cell: (612) 387-7776

Toll Free: (866) 769-8083

Email: jon@sellchology.com

Main site: Sellchology.com

Virtual Training:
SellchologyUniversity.com

Facebook: FriendSellchology.com

Twitter: FollowSellchology.com

YouTube: SellchologyTV.com

LinkedIn: ConnectWithSellchology.com

Blog: WhyCarGuy.com

Periscope: @Sellchology

Meerkat: @Sellchology

Speaker & Contributor at:

Digital Dealer Conference

Driving Sales Executive Summit

CBT News Magazine

Six Figure Auto Sales Conference

Social Proof Selling Seminar

30 Sales A Month Seminar

Automotive Super Conference

RocktoberFest Social Marketing Summit

State Association Conventions

OEM Conventions

NADA 20 Groups

NCM 20 Groups

Automotive Blogs

Six Figure Sales Strategies FB Group

Thank You ... Want something FREE?

I want to take this moment to thank you for reading the chapter on the Psychology of Selling. The word "Free" is the most powerful word in marketing if it is used by a credible source and in connection with a desirable resource, product, or service. I hope by now I have met both of these criteria.

A simple offer – Pick one:

- ✓ Free 30 minute customized webinar for your team
- ✓ Free evaluation of your recruitment and hiring process (includes ad review and 5 templates for the best recruiting ads ever written!)
- ✓ 2 Free tickets to Jonathan Dawson's next regional sales or management conference
- ✓ Free 1 month access to the Sellchology virtual training platform: www.SellchologyUniversity.com
- ✓ One Free day of on-site training with the purchase of an annual subscription to the Sellchology virtual training platform: www.SellchologyUniversity.com

Contact us and tell us what you want for FREE:

Email: info@sellchology.com
Toll free: (866) 769-8083

CHAPTER FOUR

Pick Me! Pick Me!
By David Cribbs

For those of you who are looking for that one game changing silver bullet idea that rescues your business or sends your stock soaring this probably isn't the chapter for you. However, what will be delivered in this chapter is the thought provoking idea that YOU are the silver bullet. The information shared in this chapter comes with something greater than any single idea. It comes with a responsibility. The competitive edge that I have carried throughout my career may be better described as a recognition that has been capitalized on. Recognizing what attracts and moves a customer to the point of sale and internalizing the fact that we have the ability to create those conditions is the basis of this chapter.

Becoming Attractive

For most of us, our business is dependent on our doing two things really well: gaining customers and delivering our product and or services in an exceptional way. Ultimately, we have to conquer both in order to thrive. Sounds simple enough, right? The question is how? As a trainer, I feel compelled to break it down into simple form. Let's begin with the first. How do we attract customers? Simply put, we have to become attractive and not just girl-next-door attractive; I'm talking knockdown, drag out, runway model attractive, i.e., jaw dropping, head snapping attractive! The fact is that if we can't get their attention, their undivided attention, we will never get our shot to perform.

You Had Me at Hello!

Just like Jerry Maguire, I want to have my customers at "Hello". So what's the first step in becoming this attractive to our customers? It all starts by getting sold. And once again, girl-next-door sold isn't going to cut it. You have to be SOLD OUT. This means sold on your product, your process, your management, your staff, and most of all, yourself. Let's face it, most of us get more excited and do a better job when selling someone on our favorite restaurant or movie than we do selling our own products. Imagine if we couldn't rest until our potential client had our product, not because we wanted to make a sale, but because we truly understood what the client was missing out on if they didn't have our product and service. Don't be afraid to seek some help on this one if you are not there yet. Look for others in which you see this type of conviction and start rubbing elbows. If they are genuinely sold out, they will be anxious to share with you. And if you are genuinely sold out, you will become much more attractive to your customers. Get Sold!

Confidence

Another thing that will make us attractive is confidence. Having the confidence to effectively deliver our message to the consumer is paramount. As a leader, it's your job to instill confidence in your staff. You can do this, by the way, by resorting back to the first step, being SOLD OUT! Believe in your vision and know that straying from it or compromising it will shatter confidence. Another confidence builder is training and when your staff is prepared they will be confident. If you are just getting started in your sales career, consider the speed of your development. The faster that you develop your skills, the quicker you will gain confidence. Remember that training or responding to training is your responsibility. Many of us will be fortunate enough to have support in this area, but if training is not provided to you, take action and invest in training. There are many free sources of amazing training material such as online and social forums, sponsored webinars, YouTube videos and so on. Keep in mind that ultimately the best trainers in the world are your customers. Spend as much time in front of them as possible. The final confidence builder is a victory. When you are sold out and confident in your product and service, victory is inevitable. But, in this book we are talking about having an edge so that we can experience a barrage of victories.

Creating the Conditions for the Sale

The edge that I am going to suggest, I refer to as "Creating the conditions for the sale." The ability to create the conditions for the sale begins with understanding certain things about our customers and market. What are they trying to accomplish? How do they prefer to do that? What would make it easier for them to accomplish that? What are some solutions that we can provide? How many solutions can we provide? What are some things that we can do to make all these things more easily attainable? Also, what can we implement as influencers in these areas? For example, when we know our customers are originating their searches for our product or service online, we can begin to create an amazing online experience. But it doesn't stop there. Once again, typically we are just trying to get their attention online. So, what are some specific conditions that we can create at our place of business?

The Tangibles and Intangibles

There are two basic areas of focus when it comes to creating the conditions for the sale at our physical locations. The first will be the intangibles, things like attitude, readiness and a plan of execution. The second will be the tangibles, things like décor, lighting, product placement, visual aids and the geographical layout that lends to the successful execution of our process. This will look different depending on your product or service. Being in the car business, I was recently impressed when I visited a newly built Ford store that had done exactly that. They built their store around the sales process. The geographical layout was conducive to the proven sales process that makes them successful. For me, the highlight was seeing the enclosed delivery area that the car sat in. Coincidentally, it happened to be placed behind a large glass window in the finance office where the customer finalizes the deal and contracts on the car. Imagine how this influences the customer when the eye candy of the new car is sitting right in front of them as they consider moving up another $50 or $60 per month. And the best part is that not a word has to be spoken. In that moment the car has become the salesperson by design.

Staging

Creating the conditions for the sale implies that we can be creative. Anything that we can create that will give us an edge is crucial. When I use the term edge I am talking about a legal, moral, and ethical advantage over our competition that creates a better overall experience for the customer and us. Just like in the example above, staging is an easy condition for us to create. When you visit a model home, it is typically furnished in a very strategic manner that lends to the potential of the home and leaves less to the imagination while creating the feelings that the seller is attempting to stir up in the potential buyer. In supermarkets, product placement is a science. The eye level shelf space sells more than the higher or lower shelves. The same types of products are always near the checkout registers for a purpose. In the car business, I like to have digital photo frames on the salespersons' desks that constantly scroll through all of the positive things that we offer as value propositions including accolades, community involvement, and personal pictures of salespeople and customers. This helps us to deliver our message to the customer without opening our mouths. Once again, we have a device selling by design.

Appointments

Another opportunity to create additional conditions comes with the appointment. Everyone loves an appointment because we know that our closing ratios move upward. Now we have additional opportunities to raise those ratios even higher by creating additional conditions. Again using the car business as an example, the appointment gives us the opportunity to create several conditions ahead of time. The most obvious is having a vehicle prepared to show the customer. But, we are looking for an edge, right? So, let's take this further. Let's begin by googling our customer's name. Yeah, let's find out more about them, if possible. Imagine learning that your customer is a real estate agent, for example. This gives us an immediate connection after they arrive. We may even have a referral for them before we get started. Do you think that may get their attention? We can also have third party evaluations of their trade pre-printed in the event that we need them as a closing tool. This will save time and you will appear more professional, once again separating you from the crowd. The final condition that I will suggest is a third party introduction upon your guest's arrival. Avoid waiting outside or even standing in the showroom in anticipation of your customer's arrival. Go to your desk prior to your appointment and coordinate an introduction at your desk using the receptionist or a partner. This is not only a professional move, but it puts the customer seated at your desk for the initial interview.

Online Presence

Now that we are becoming more attractive through our preparation and readiness to execute in an exceptional way, how do we get in front of customers for them to notice our striking attributes? Again, for many of us, most of our initial first impressions will be made online. As important as it is to have a great looking and functioning website, once again we need an edge and this is arguably the most important place right now to have one. We have managed to fill our sites with plenty of helpful information and we have even been able to move most of our sales process there. But what is the most important part of any sales process and the most difficult to create online? It's rapport. Ah, that magical thing called rapport. Imagine the online impact if we could somehow pull this one off. Let's take a look at what that would look like.

Transparency

When your customers are on your site they are forming an opinion or imagining what it may be like at your physical location. Why leave it to their imagination when we have the ability to bring it to them? Most of our potential online customers' anxiety lies in wondering whom they will be dealing with and how they will be dealt with. Why not take these anxieties away right from the start. Specifically, we need to have video on our sites. Even more specifically, we need to have video of our personnel, preferably in action. Show your people doing what they do, not acting, but performing their actual duties. Show off their personalities and there vulnerabilities. Include your management team in this and fill up your site with raw footage. Transparency and reality sell. It's now a big part of our culture and future and if I find it on your site that's where I will be hanging out.

Customer Acquisition

Since we are in customer acquisition mode, let's talk about some other ways to find new customers. As elusive as they may seem at times, they can be methodically tracked. One of the ways we can do this is by determining who has joint custody of our potential customers. For example, if you are in car sales there are several other related industries that share custody at peak potential times such as body shops, insurance agents, credit unions and more. We can form strategic alliances with many of these businesses. Remember that we bring as much value to them as they do to us, and thankfully, most others just won't take the time to pursue these relationships! By being in more places, we can attract more customers. And by attracting more customers we create the opportunities to perform, or should I say, outperform any others.

Action

Has anyone noticed that I keep throwing this one word around "create or creating"? It's no coincidence that this word keeps appearing and it's no coincidence that it happens to be an action word. Yes, I finally said the "A" word. Ultimately, those who are the most ravishing are those who are taking the most action when it comes to creating opportunities. As important as it is to plan, strategize, and prepare, there is absolutely nothing stronger or more attractive than taking action. In today's market, fast is the new big. While most are planning to reach out to a customer, you should have already scheduled the appointment. I recently visited a site and while I was on the site my phone was ringing with a representative from that company. And yes, I was impressed. Any planning or system that you have in place when it comes to responding to an opportunity should have played out prior to the opportunity arising. This is why we call it planning or preparing or why we refer to it as a system or process. If we haven't created the conditions for the sale prior to having the opportunity, now we are either delaying our response to the customer while we create a plan or strategy or we are just gun slinging or shooting from the hip and our process and the customer's experience looks different each time. Creating the conditions for the sale allows us to respond immediately and meet the customer right where they are in the sales process and allows us to consistently respond appropriately and impressively.

The Moment of Truth

Now, let's move forward to the point in which the customer is in front of us. This is the moment of truth. Do we have the personality to match our dashing looks? In other words, do we have the skills to provide the consistency of the experience in-person? Remember that in one way or another we attracted the customer. How do we know that? We know that because they showed up. They are there and they may or may not be expecting the consistency, but they are most certainly hoping for it. The last thing that we want to do is open our mouths only to become a disappointment. A great salesperson has already internalized this fact and is prepared to deliver. Customers have a unique ability to sniff out our motives, and dare I say, tactics. An amazing barometer of our intentions can be measured by asking ourselves "Are we looking for the buyer?" If so, we are more than likely selling the customer experience short. The number one reason that franchises like McDonalds are so successful is the consistency in which they deliver their product and service. There is a comfort level in seeing the same big "M" no matter where you are on the planet and knowing that the Big Mac and fries are going to be the same. Even New Car franchise dealers have been mandated to build facilities that look the same to provide that branding comfort. The point is that if we find ourselves looking for the buyer when we have a prospect in front of us, we will begin to alter our process and presentation instead of relying on it. Aren't we supposed to be SOLD OUT?

Execution

There is just no way to put this gently. We just cannot fail here. This is what we have prepared for, the opportunity to lead the customer to a favorable decision on their behalf, and yes, I said on THEIR behalf. It's okay because this is not reflective of any profit margins. It's just a fact that until your customer feels good about what they are getting, you will not have a deal. If we get a deal, it means that someone approved it on our behalf as well. The big question when it comes to execution takes us back to the beginning of the chapter when our first step to becoming attractive was to become SOLD OUT! You see, when you are sold out you are unencumbered by the facts. When the customer has a concern or an objection, rely on your training and your process to navigate through. You don't stop and throw your hands up in the air and give up or respond in a less than positive way. Your training has taught you to be understanding, in agreement with your customer, and ready to provide a solution for them that acknowledges their concern. And sometimes it is just that, just acknowledging. So yeah, we have to perform in an amazing way if we want to excel in this business. A friend recently said that ultimately if you can't land a fighter jet on a carrier in the middle of the ocean then you can't be a navy fighter pilot. We are no different. We have to land the plane.

Customer Retention

Think about our typical customer retention strategies. Is it calling the customer when it's close to renewal time? Maybe it's giving them a little something special to keep them from leaving. If we truly examine our retention strategies, I think we will find the majority of them unimpressive, if we even have any in place. And although I would never suggest that you abandon any of these measures, they would become nothing more than a formality if we truly had our customers at "Hello".

At the beginning of this chapter, I mentioned that the success of our business was contingent upon doing only two things really well, gaining customers and delivering our product or services in an exceptional way. You may have noticed the omission of retention. I'm challenging the theory that this is a third category, because if we believe in the first two, we get the third as a bonus. Imagine our winning proposition being so powerful that we are simultaneously creating a losing one- Creating such a consumer experience that anything less than what we offer would be a loss for our customer. It is no secret that in the car business the stakes are high when it comes to customer satisfaction and each new car customer receives a survey after the sale that impacts our incomes. In the car business, we are typically trained to coach or remind the customer as to the importance and impact of this survey and I am not going to suggest that you change your process. What I will share with you is that this was an area that I consistently excelled in when I was on the sales floor selling vehicles and yet I rarely ever mentioned the survey to my customers. The survey always took a backseat to the true experience that I was obsessed with creating for my customers. When we are truly creating this type of experience, we understand that our customer retention strategy occurred when we said "Hello" and continues each day.

Opportunity

When writing the final section of this chapter I originally titled the section "Conclusion". As I reflected on the opening statements of this chapter, I concluded very quickly that the title had to change. In the opening statements, the disclaimer was that this chapter would come with a responsibility. That responsibility is making a decision. You can decide to check this chapter off as another one read or you can gain an edge in your business by becoming more attractive, creating the conditions for the sale and performing in a way that your customers would be disappointed by any other experience that your competitors could provide. Remember, YOU are the silver bullet!

BIO: DAVID CRIBBS
Lead Trainer, Auto Dealer University
Co-Host, Auto Dealer Live

David is the Lead Trainer for Auto Dealer University and the Co-Host of Auto Dealer Live. David began his career in 1989 selling new Toyotas and rose through the ranks becoming the BDC Internet Manager and New Car Manager with Toyota. In 2001 David left Toyota and assisted in the opening of a very successful staffed event direct mail company. David traveled for approximately 5 years as a Closer and Trainer at staffed events across the country. In 2006 David accepted a position as a New/Used Car Manager for Nissan. In 2010, David partnered as an owner/operator of an independent automobile and motorcycle dealership. In February of 2014 David joined Imperial Press Direct as the Corporate Trainer and Lead Trainer of Auto Dealer University and also serves as the Co-Host of Auto Dealer Live "The Show Where Dealers Go".

Contact Information:
David Cribbs

3104 Cherry Palm Drive, Suite 220
Tampa, FL 33619

Cell: 813-463-4041
Office: 813-630-5888
Fax: 813-630-1048

Email: dcribbs@imperialpressdirect.com

www.imperialpressdirect.com

AUTO Ⓤ DEALER
UNIVERSITY

"Success from within"

Classic training. Modern application. Transforming dealerships.

- ➤ **Custom Training Plans**
- ➤ **Curriculum/Testing**
- ➤ **Interactive Training**
- ➤ **Individual Tracking**
- ➤ **Industry Leading Trainers**
- ➤ **24/7 Access**

" With the tools and training provided by ADU, you will master sales, service and BDC development. "

Ready to Become a Closer? Contact us today!

✉ info@autodealeruniversity.net

📞 844-415-1053

🌐 www.autodealeruniversity.net

CHAPTER FIVE

HOW (to gain a competitive advantage)

By John Brown

In this chapter let's explore a rather simple, yet complex idea of HOW. Most people spend a life time never thinking about an everyday used term like how. It might be used as a noun, a verb, an adverb, a conjunction. It could be an acronym, Hope, Opportunity and Willingness is a great description. So far in my career How has stood the test of time as being defined as in what way or manner, by what means.

The realization that the HOW in your life defines your success and failures. It defines and gives purpose to the more often asked terms like what and why. Business leaders across the planet have realized that the answer to HOW can set them apart. It can give them the competitive advantage they need to succeed.

Regardless of the type of dealership or business you operate, maximizing your potential to produce results and your discovery of HOW will set you apart from your direct and indirect competitors. Follow me through the journey of the discovery of HOW that has changed my life and the people and organizations that I have been blessed with that have touched my life and made me better. Your answers to How will give you that competitive advantage which will separate you from all the rest.

Growing up in a small town, Columbus, Indiana, USA was good for me. I had no idea that I was poor compared to many of my friends. I didn't feel poor. I grew up in a loving household with great parents- a stay at home mom who was always there for us and a hard working father who owned and operated the first local supermarket. My older brother went to work in the grocery store before he graduated from high school, and me, well, I did one summer there and another at the local foundry pouring hot cast iron for diesel engine blocks and instantly understood that I wanted to be the first in my family to graduate from college and not have to work in either place.

Fortunately, I had a couple of options for college. I was a pretty good athlete in high school. I lettered in three different sports, football, swimming and track for a total of eight out of nine varsity letters. I was the second fastest kid in town and about twice the size of the fastest guy. So there was interest from some college football coaches. Indiana University and Lee Corso recruited me. My high school football coach played on the 1968 IU Rose Bowl team and was pushing me to go to IU. The Air Force Academy recruited me as well.

In the end, I enrolled at Ball State University. It was farther from home than IU but not as far away as Colorado Springs. Go figure, I decided to play rugby in college. A hometown friend and a starter on the university basketball team recruited me to join the Sigma Chi Fraternity. I knew nothing about the Greek letter organizations. Looking back, this was my first brush with HOW.

During my junior year, spring quarter, I read in the daily campus newspaper an advertisement about being an intern in the Indiana State Senate. Wow, that sounded interesting, I thought. I was a marketing major, never grew up around politics. Didn't even have an idea if my parents were Republicans or Democrats. But it sounded interesting. So I called and asked for an interview.

I later found out that I was the last person to be interviewed and there were about 80 others before me. Great, I thought; this can't be good. But I went ahead and showed up. I had absolutely no idea what to expect. I took one class in political science, the mandatory basic requirements for graduation, and had no experience whatsoever in politics. One thing was for sure, I had signed up and my parents had always insisted that if I signed up for anything…scouts, sports…I could not quit. I had to finish what I started. So I went to the interview.

When I arrived at the BSU Student Center for my interview, the director of the program introduced himself to me and we sat down. He was in a suit and tie and very official looking. I didn't even own a suit. From the beginning, there was no small talk. We just launched right in. First question, "Do you happen to know who your state senator is?" he asked. Pause.

As a matter of fact, I did know who it was, basically because his daughter was a friend from high school.

Next question, "Can you name either your US Congressman or your US Senator?" Another pause.

Well, as a matter of fact, I did know. You see, the US Congressman lived about a block away from me at home, and as for my US Senator, two of his sons were in my fraternity and one was in my pledge class. Can you say LUCKY?!

"Thank you very much and I will be in touch," he said. I stood up and shook his hand and walked back to the fraternity house. Good thing it was a Thursday and I could look forward to a function with one of the campus sororities that night because what I just experienced in that interview was my second introduction to HOW.

A week or so went by and I got a letter from the State of Indiana Senate in the mail. It was very official and impressive with the gold State seal on it. I said to myself, here is the rejection letter. I opened it up and to my complete surprise, it was a letter welcoming me to the internship. I had been selected along with about a dozen others to be an intern for four months in the Indiana State Senate. I had to attend a week long, mandatory orientation over Christmas break and would begin my assignment on January 2nd.

After the orientation and assignment to my senator, I had to write him a letter and introduce myself. Mission completed. I received a quick response from my letter to the senator and his letter took me completely off guard. I was expecting an official response from a person who was an elected official. This senator was a big time state senator, chairman of one of the most important and powerful committees, and a member of the leadership team. That wasn't the kind of letter I received. It wasn't necessarily what he said; it was HOW he said it.

It's January 1980 and I'm interning in the Indiana Senate- a small town boy, no political background, and no real involvement with politics, until now. There's nothing like learning to swim in the deep end, so to speak. What I would learn about the legislative process wasn't to be found in a college textbook. This wasn't academia; this was raw politics in real time. I loved it.

Toward the end of the session, the senator that sat next to my assigned senator approached me. He introduced himself, told me that he had spoken to the senator I worked for and that he had told him that I was one of the best interns he had ever had. This particular state senator had decided to run for lt. governor and wanted me to join his campaign and work for him.

Fast forward to November of 1980 and the Reagan landside was felt in Indiana. Not only did Reagan win the presidency, but the governor and lieutenant governor team won as well. I was asked if I wanted to come to work in the State Capitol. At the time, across the USA, there was high unemployment, no economic growth, twenty one and a half percent interest rates, the misery index was the highest ever and most of my fraternity brothers didn't have jobs yet, so I jumped at the chance to have a job.

Not long after being in office, along about April, we were told that the Vice President of the United States was coming to Indianapolis to visit a friend of his, the mayor of Indianapolis, and would be stopping by the State House to see the governor and lieutenant governor prior to his visit to the mayor's office. The day of the vice president's visit, while the VP, the governor and the lieutenant governor met inside the governor's office, a member of the VP's staff casually asked me if I would ever consider working for the VP. He presented me with his business card and asked me to forward my resume to him.

Yea, right. Me? Work for the Vice President of the United States? A kid who grew up on the wrong side of the tracks in Columbus, Indiana, and who didn't know any better and thought he was just like any other kid in town? No way. This guy was a professional. He probably passed out a box of business cards every other day. I got in my head that I wasn't going to stoop to that level and send my resume to be told "thanks, but no thanks." I was already living a dream life. No way was I going to send him my resume!

The lady I was dating at the time, now my wife of 33 years, kept asking me each and every day if I had sent my resume to the VP's office. Finally, some five months later, just to get her to quit asking, I sent my resume to the name and address on the business card.

It seemed that within hours after sending in my resume, I got a phone call about interviewing. I had to go out to Santa Fe, New Mexico, to interview. It seemed that the vice president had a visit scheduled there and that was the fastest way to get the ball rolling. Long story short, I am now working for THE vice president.

HOW?

During the Staff Christmas party at the vice president's residence after the victorious campaign of 1984, The Honorable Vice President took my wife aside, who was visibly pregnant with our first child, and reminded her that he had done his part in letting me go home for at least one night during the long campaign. For my wife, living again in Washington DC where she grew up was an answered prayer. I was still a small town kid from Indiana and still a little gun-shy of the Washington establishment. After our son was born in the spring, I got a phone call from the governor of Indiana and was told that it was time to come back home to Indiana. To my wife's dismay, we headed back to the governor's office for an opportunity that would keep one foot firmly planted with the vice president's office and one foot with the governor's office.

With the election of President George H. W. Bush in 1988, the president selected the governor of Indiana to become the US Ambassador to Singapore. HOW did that happen you might ask?

During the election cycle of 1988, I realized that as long as you are winning elections, things are great, but if you lose, then what? What would my family do if I didn't have a job? So I decided that I needed to try to leverage what I knew into a private sector job. This led to an opportunity through a friend of mine with EDS, with Ross Perot. I joined the Government Affairs team to start the State and Local Government Affairs practice in Washington, DC, and so back to DC we went.

Nearly three years later and out of nowhere, I got a phone call from a friend of mine from high school whose father was the CEO of Arvin, a FORTUNE 250 Company in the automotive parts business. He asked me if on my next trip home to see my parents, I could phone him and try to visit while in town. I did and he shared with me his vision to take Arvin, a $300 million dollar company that supplied the Big Three in Detroit and turn it into a global leader in the automotive sector. This was my introduction to HOW.

He told me that he needed me to help him accomplish his vision. While I knew him as the father of a friend, Mr. Baker as I would call him because my mother would absolutely go crazy if I called him Jim as he requested, had spent his entire career building this company. From the mailroom to the CEO's office, this incredible businessman had a vision. I didn't know a thing about what he wanted me to do, but he insisted he could teach me. He knew I could excel at the job, he said, because he had observed from my brief youthful career up to now, that I could make happen the HOW to make his company into the global leader.

In just about 10 years, we turned the company into a truely global supplier and one of the top ten largest auto parts companies in the World. But then, Mr. Baker retired and new leadership decided in a new direction. I was now faced for the first time with not the HOW, but why. I could figure out the HOW and I did my job to accomplish a merger of equals between Arvin and Meritor. But I couldn't get the right answers as to WHY this was a good idea. I was struggling with HOW to be an officer of the company.

So, I decided to move on. I would use everything I learned about HOW, and land my dream job with Rolls-Royce. This opportunity was a combination of everything I had done throughout my career to date- investor relations, government relations, media relations, visual communications, community relations, employee communications, branding and public relations. I understood the HOW. Rolls-Royce understood HOW. Everything was a dream come true. Then a phone call came out of the blue. A friend of a friend wanted me to come to Charlotte.

Charlotte had changed a lot. When I first started going to Charlotte in the early 1990's, the downtown area, which Charlotteans call "Uptown" was not a pretty site. Nothing happened after five o'clock in the afternoon and many of the storefronts were boarded up. The leadership in Charlotte decided to change all of that and turn Charlotte into one of the best communities across the US in which to live and work.

As a family, we decided to move to Charlotte. My next dream job was about to become a reality. One rarely happens, but more than one dream job during the same career? HOW lucky can you be? Not lucky, as I learned. You just have to understand HOW.

The Carolinas Independent Automobile Dealers Association (CIADA), over the last 60 years, has been the leading organization that represents the independent dealers across many audiences. Most recently, the CIADA is among the leading organizations not only on the state level, but nationally as well. On the state level, the entire board is engaged in transformation leadership for the organization.

On a national basis, we have significant human capital invested by multiple board members. Most recently, the National Quality Dealer of the Year Award and the National Community Service Award were awarded to two CIADA Board members, Darla Booher and Michael Darrow, respectively. These two independent dealers are leaders in their communities. In addition, they are single handedly and collectively changing proving that used car dealers are among the best business people. They understand HOW.

So what's behind all this HOW stuff? It isn't rocket science or brain surgery. It's the ability to look at anything and ask yourself, "HOW?" Not "Why" or "When", not "If" or "Should", but "HOW". Businesses don't fail, dealerships don't fail, and nothing fails on its own. People fail. That isn't necessarily a bad thing. Failure leads to success. When you examine the HOW, and you make it a core principle, you begin to achieve the results you desire.

Let me give you one example before I go back and explain the HOW in this chapter of the book. It is not a surprise to anyone who knows me that I am a huge fan of Chick Fil A. Maybe some would say I'm a fanatic. I think they would be right! The founder of CFA didn't start out to build the multi-billion dollar restaurant chain that would become the largest seller of chicken in the world. Yes, larger than KFC. As he explains in his book, he started out with only one goal in mind, to take care of his family. He understood that the HOW was to "flip burgers and chicken". He went on to selling "chicken fillets" on the menu, to Chick Fil A where the "A" stands for Grade A. CFA understands HOW!

My understanding of HOW came about when the CEO of ARVIN hired me and became my mentor. I would spend many, many hours in the "Principal's" office (the Headquarters of Arvin was actually in an old school house and the CEO's office was in one of the old classrooms) where we would work on countless strategic plans for growth, for products, and for everything we did in the business. It didn't matter if it was the minutest thing, you could think of in a business, eventually the conversation would end up at HOW.

HOW would we achieve what we wanted? Yes, the strategic plan played a role with goals and objectives, strengths and weaknesses, KPI's, Six Sigma etc., etc., but we always started and ended with HOW. In the end, the HOW was always an indication of what was a success or failure. HOW did we succeed or HOW did that fail?

Let's go back. Now I started to understand my first brushes with HOW…HOW did I end up at Ball State, HOW did I end up a member of Sigma Chi?

HOW did I end up becoming a State Senate Intern?

HOW did I get that job on the first campaign?

HOW did I end up as a staff member of the Vice President of the United States?

HOW did I end up at EDS, ARVIN, Rolls-Royce and CIADA?

HOW did I end up doing lots of other things I haven't even discussed, like getting elected to four terms on the city council?

HOW is the current governor of Indiana a good friend of mine? HOW do I know the current governor of North Carolina and countless others in my life?

It's all about the personal relationship. Let's examine the idea of HOW more closely.

I ended up at Ball State because of my relationship with my father and his company's headquarters, which were located in Muncie, Indiana.

I ended up as a member of Sigma Chi Fraternity because of a fellow Columbus student taking me under his wing and asking me to join his fraternity.

I ended up as an intern because I was one of the only interviewees who knew their elected representatives. HOW did I know mine? I knew because I had a personal experience with all of them. They were friends or they lived three houses down the street or they were pledge brothers of mine.

HOW did I get to work for one of the most influential members of the Indiana General Assembly? While neither of us knew each other, he was a Sigma Chi from another chapter and we had experienced a personal relationship via the Fraternity.

HOW did I end up working for the lieutenant governor Candidate? Because of a personal trust he had with the senator I was working for.

HOW did I end up working for the Vice President of the United States? I later learned that the guy who gave me his business card had never done that before. He said it was based on a personal conversation he had with me earlier in the evening that I still to this day don't remember.

Why did the vice president allow me to work on his staff? Because of the relationship he had with the governor. He could have hired anyone.

Why did I get the opportunity with Ross Perot and EDS? Because of a personal relationship I had with a mutual friend who recommended me.

Why did I get a phone call from the CEO of Arvin? It was because I knew his daughter.

HOW did I get the opportunity of a lifetime with Rolls-Royce? Because of a relationship I had with a former Congressman who was also a former Indiana State Senator and now the Government affairs VP for Rolls-Royce.

I even ended up in Charlotte because of the relationships I had developed over my career. Some would call it luck. And I would agree being in the right place at the right time is important. But it is also about the HOW.

The same holds true with CIADA. The relationships between the dealers and the vendors, the regulators and legislators, make CIADA one of the most powerful organizations for the independent used car dealer.

The success of your dealership is all based on HOW you decide to run your car lot. HOW do you build relationships? Do you want a relationship with all your customers or just some of them? HOW are you going to operate? HOW are you going to grow your dealership? HOW are you going to make sure you are in compliance, not just today, but every day? HOW are you going to form partnerships with floor planners, finance companies and service contract providers?

HOW will you grow personally in your role at the dealership? HOW will you stand out? HOW will you stay pulled-in? HOW will you deliver superior customer service and a customer experience that is second to none? HOW will you make sure the people who work for you share the same vision and values for your organization that you have?

The sum total of all your HOWs is your reputation. Reputation is what you stand for. Can you be trusted? What is your track record of accomplishments? It's HOW others think of you.

Reputation can take a lifetime to build and only moments to lose. It's a valid indicator of your ability to build and sustain success. It's a value that is earned by you, but given by others.

In today's connected society, your company's reputation is also more directly related to your employees' reputations because they are the face of the organization. If they don't share the same vision of HOW, then your entire organization is at risk. The company's reputation is therefore based on the customer experiences from everyone in the organization and the trust that is encountered. No longer will a company's reputation supersede or outweigh that of its employees.

We live in a highly transparent and instant communications world, so customers know when there's a disconnect between the company and its employees. It is primarily because the employee will be the conduit to the world about your business. HOW we choose employees to be part of our organization and your team has never been more important. Therefore, reputational capital is real and worth the investment.

My mention of one of my previous employers is worth expanding on in regards to reputational capital. Rolls-Royce is undoubtedly one of the most recognizable and valuable brands in the world. For more than a century their brand has been synonymous with trust, quality, excellence and an emotional bond with the customer. Rolls-Royce is one of the most famous brands in the world, primarily known for the car it no longer even makes. The brand is also one of its most valuable assets. It opens doors, attracts talented people, reassures customers, and gives them the credibility to move into new markets.

The Rolls-Royce brand never stops evolving. The company leadership understands this and has built a culture throughout the organization of employees who want to maintain and grow with it. That is why the company goes to great lengths with everything it does to answer the question, HOW? Rolls-Royce understands the difference between building a brand that everyone knows vs. a brand that everyone trusts. Rolls-Royce knows the difference between delivering superior customer service and providing customer experience. They work every minute of every hour of every day of every year to earn a reputation that provides a value-added proposition.

When Rolls-Royce gets it wrong, it spends whatever it takes to answer the question, "HOW did it go wrong?" Wrong only becomes a failure when the company doesn't learn HOW to fix what went wrong. Employees celebrate, literally, finding fixes to problems. The Rolls-Royce culture provides for extraordinary learning which empowers the individual. Therefore, Rolls-Royce is Trusted to Deliver Excellence in every aspect of its business. It all begins with the simple prospect of HOW.

You are now thinking that this all sounds great, but my dealership isn't Rolls-Royce. I don't have the resources of a Rolls-Royce or an Arvin or even a large independent car dealership. What you have to remember is that Rolls-Royce didn't start out being what they are today. That holds true for everyone. Apple wasn't even around in 1975. FaceBook, Walmart, and every other business you can name, all started with that first employee. They built a business and a reputation with their employees and customers to get where they are today. Those who ignored the HOW, are no longer with us. Remember Hummer, PAN AM Airlines, Circuit City, DeLorian, Borders, Oldsmobile and the list goes on and on.

HOW will you build the reputation of your company? Your customers are going to know all about your dealership and the cars on your lot long before they ever step foot on your lot. Today's technology drives consumers, from grandparents to generation Z just now beginning their working careers, to find you electronically. If they can't find you, or if prior consumers have posted horrifying experiences, you simply lose out. Managing the HOW of your dealership is more important than ever. HOW will your Dealership become extraordinary?

Regardless of the type of business you are in, your future depends on one simple term, HOW. Your ability to have your customer see you differently and want to conduct commerce with you ensures continued success. Your pursuit of excellence, your employee's future and your personal success will be determined by HOW you do what you are going to do.

Statistics indicate the measurement of how well you are engaging the HOW. In today's business climate, if every business in your vertical is doing generally the same thing, the one who spends the most money wins. Most can't afford that business plan. The HOW can set you apart.

The best of the best by almost any business measurement you use, ROI, profit, sales, compensation, inventory turns, energy consumed, cost of quality, waste or miles driven have mastered the how. The only question left to ask is to you. How do you want to proceed?

Take the next step. Figure out the HOW in your life. It all starts with a plan. Not a good idea, not a thought process or a concept. A plan. Put your how into a written plan. Simply start by answering this question…HOW am I going to…provide for my family, build a company, make a million dollars?

HOW do I know you'll succeed? Because those who have accomplished and mastered the HOW in their lives have demonstrated time and again that those who grasp the concept of their own HOW, succeed.

The only HOW in my life that I can't figure out is the "HOW did I get cancer" question? Someday I'm hopeful that doctors and researchers who are all much smarter than I will know the answer to this question. I hope so, because when they figure that out, I'll have a better chance at living life longer. But until then, I am assured that even the very best and brightest who are working on a cure for cancer, are asking themselves- HOW?

BIO: JOHN BROWN
Executive Director, CIADA

John Brown currently serves as the Executive Director of CIADA. In this capacity, John is responsible for all aspects of the member-driven association. As a results-driven executive with experience at global automotive organizations, John also has a long and accomplished history in philanthropy and government relations as a trusted advisor to elected officials, corporate and non-profit executives.

John served as director of corporate communications for Rolls-Royce Corporation. At Rolls-Royce, John was responsible for integrated marketing communications, including internal and external communications, media relations, trade shows and exhibits, state and local government relations, community relations, branding, visual communications and corporate social responsibility. He was the lead communications executive on the crisis communications planning and implementation committee, as well as, the primary spokesperson for Rolls-Royce. John served on the board of the political action committee (PAC) and was responsible for corporate social responsibility (CSR) planning and contributions.

Earlier, John served as a corporate officer and vice president for Arvin Inc. (ArvinMeritor), one of the largest global automotive parts manufacturers with more than half of its revenues and profits derived from outside of the United States. At Arvin, John was responsible for integrating investor relations, marketing, corporate communications, public relations, community relations, government relations, graphics and public affairs on a global basis. As the top Investor Relations executive for the Company, John was instrumental in helping grow the Company from $350 million to over $7.5 billion. John also served as the President of the Arvin Foundation.

Active in the community, John was elected to four terms on the city council and served as president of the City Council. In addition, he sat on the boards of the Columbus Housing Authority, United Way, Boys and Girls Club, Habitat for Humanity and New American Schools.

After graduating from Ball State University, John started his career by serving in the offices of the Indiana Lt. Governor and Governor; and as a staff member to the Vice-President of the United States, The Honorable George H.W. Bush. John also served on the re-election campaign staff for Reagan-Bush in 1984. Following the election of George H.W. Bush as President of the United States, Indiana's Governor, the Honorable Bob Orr, was named Ambassador to Singapore where John continued to serve as a trusted advisor.

John, and his wife, Katherine, have three grown children. William, lives in Washington DC. Martha and Margaret both live and work in Charlotte, NC. He enjoys yard work, growing more than 45 varieties of hostas and researching his family's history. John is a cancer survivor since 2011 and continues to serve others as an outspoken advocate and fundraiser for cancer research.

Contact Information:
John Brown
Carolinas Independent Automobile Dealers Association
P: (800) 432-4232   E: jbrown@theciada.com

CAROLINAS INDEPENDENT
AUTOMOBILE DEALERS ASSOCIATION

"The only non-profit association representing independent automobile dealers in the Carolinas".

Industry Lobbying/Governmental Affairs
Representation with DMV in North and South Carolina
Dealer Education
Garage Liability Insurance
Dealer Bonds
Dealer Forms
Other Related Dealership Services

"We're On Your Team!"

www.TheCIADA.com
(800) 432-4232 Toll Free
(704) 455-2117 Office

CHAPTER SIX

This is no longer your daddy's car business or is it?

By Michael Samaan

When I began working in my family's used car business, marketing on the Internet was unheard of, as in, it didn't exist. Advertising our inventory consisted of placing ads in the local newspaper or pennysaver, and purchasing radio or local TV airtime. If someone was interested in a car on the lot, they might have shopped us against a few local dealers, but that was about it. Treat them right, sell them a good quality car at a fair price, and former customers would bring us more potential customers who were searching for a particular vehicle. And, they trusted us to find it for them. If they had a problem with the car, they came back and we worked with them to make it right.

Whether we like it or not, the Internet has now changed the way buyers think and act. More and more consumers are turning to social media, smart phone apps and web sites, thoroughly researching their intended purchase before actually making a buying decision, no matter the car location. This doesn't necessarily mean that consumers are any smarter than before. The information is just so readily available and easily accessible that anyone can pretend to be an expert. One thing is for certain. This societal push towards technology is changing the consumer purchasing and research process. Applying new concepts to your business either through general process modification or through new technology is a constantly evolving animal. The use of new technology is becoming indispensable but it's equally important not to lose touch with the basics. Ultimately, customers still want to see and touch their intended purchase and still need the human connection. Technology has made basic customer service all the more important. Technology can and should be viewed as a tool to enhance and promote great customer service, not as an alternative to it.

Please don't be afraid of change

One of the cool parts of my current job in charge of dealer operations for Auto Data Direct, is that I get to attend meetings and conventions all over the United States. I am fortunate to be in front of many top industry experts. My background allows for an added benefit when hearing about new concepts and programs because I understand, from a practical standpoint, what new products can actually help a dealer. When I ran my dealerships, we participated in developing current sales applications that are now starting to emerge. To see where these applications have gone in such a short time is mind blowing. The proof is in the pudding. Just watch what the large operators are doing. Trust me. If a large, publicly traded dealer group is utilizing a new technology that a vendor is offering, you can bet a lot of practical and economic research went into that decision.

Don't be afraid of this change. Fear of anything new is a death nail in today's rapidly changing, web-based, smart-phone-driven world. Fear is the reactionary defense mechanism that springs to life anytime someone suggests a new business idea or way of doing things. Whenever a new idea is presented, inevitably you will hear the response from somebody "That's not the way we've done it in the past". Just take time to listen and think through each proposition. Imagine its application in your business, and research the process before you make that judgment call.

One of the new rapidly growing web-based services is Electronic Lien & Title (ELT). The concept of a lienholder having their titles residing in the digital ether rather than in paper form sitting in a locked filing cabinet in the back office at the car lot is scary to many independent financers. Growing up around Buy-Here Pay-Here (BHPH) dealers I can certainly understand their initial hesitation. After all, that special piece of secure paper represents a tangible investment, but truth be told, the ELT process takes away a lot of the burden associated with housing and maintaining all those months and years of accumulated paper titles. With a central electronic database that can be queried by multiple resources, it is also less likely there will be instances of title lien fraud. After the lienholder sends the electronic satisfy message, depending on the state, the responsibility of mailing the satisfied paper titles to customers is now shifted to the state agency or contracted state agent for processing.

We have a BHPH dealer client who I have known since I was a teenager. They have been in business for almost 40 years using basically the same title management and payment collection process- a 100-yr old safe and a box of index cards! When ELT became mandatory, it was one of the first of many frantic phone calls that I received. Needless to say, they were not happy with the new concept and waited until after the mandatory start date had passed and they had been turned away from the DMV when attempting to record their paper liens. Refusing to buy a computer and pay for Internet service, they chose to use the computer at the library to satisfy their liens and order their paper titles. One day I noticed by their lien and registration totals that their business was doing pretty well. When I visited their store about a year after the ELT implementation, they had finally made peace with the new process, bought a computer, and even had an Internet connection. Interestingly enough they had also had their grandson create a website for them that contained pictures of their inventory taken and posted with their new smartphone! They were still hesitant to admit it, but technology had actually helped make their business process easier.

Auto dealers are a savvy and aggressive bunch. From maintaining interactive web sites and social media marketing to diversifying their ever-changing inventory and keeping up with the wants of their clientele, dealers are constantly reinventing. Still it amazes me to see clients who do not maintain a website or post their inventory online. Some dealers have their head buried in the sand, but digital marketing is not going away. Buy-here Pay-here dealers give excuses that their customers don't shop them against other dealers. Many of them come by referral and they "take any car we put them in for $500.00 down and $50.00 per week". While this is certainly true of a certain segment of BHPH customers, savvy buyers are even shopping digitally between BHPH lots. More and more BHPH customers can and do shop around and are being sought after even by franchise dealers who after going through the automotive down turn in 2008-2009 were forced to try and retail everything they could, squeeze as much profit out of every car possible and use all available avenues to get customers riding. As a result, many of them turned to deep, subprime and even in-house financing.

Regardless of your business, technology is forcing change. Some will go kicking and screaming along the way, however, the integration of technology into our daily lives, regardless of our social class, is increasing every day. Personal banking is mostly performed online and payments can now be made at the local sandwich shop by waving your smart phone over a pad. According to statisticbrain.com, by 2015 projected U.S. online sales will exceed $340B, more than doubling sales from 2009. Let's face it: technology is no longer the exception; it is the rule.

Complacency is a killer
Being in the retail car business my entire adult life, I was blind to what customers actually had to go through not only in purchasing a vehicle but in having it serviced, until about six years ago when I had to buy my first car from the other side

of the desk. Like many consumers today, I took interest in a certified pre-owned car that I had found online. The price was fair and it had the mileage and options that I was looking for. When I pulled up to the dealership, I got out of my car and started hunting for the car on the lot. After about 5 minutes, I found the car I saw online. Fifteen minutes later as I wandered around looking over other options on the lot, there was still no salesperson in sight. I thought, wow, everyone must be busy. This was a franchise store with 200 cars on the ground; it's just abnormal not to be mauled by a salesman the moment you get out of your car, right? I decided to walk inside where it was cool and wait. However, as I walked into the showroom, right past three salespeople under the service entrance overhang smoking cigarettes, I saw the sales manager sitting in his office completely disengaged behind his computer screen. There was a receptionist in the middle of the showroom typing what appeared to be a school paper. Neither of these individuals even acknowledged my presence. I shook my head, turned around and went right back out the door. If this buying experience started out this way, it surely wasn't going to end any better. Obviously this was an extreme example of complacency; but while some dealerships are reluctant to enter the technology age, others are relying so much on the Internet to drive their traffic that they are becoming complacent when it comes to actually taking care of the customer.

Over my lifetime, I have been involved with many car dealerships, so I realize each store has its unique personality. Sometimes you can feel the lack of identity or direction with a store and its employees just by walking on the lot. Customers are already hesitant about walking on your lot and going through the sales process, so, if your environment doesn't feel inviting it will make it that much more difficult to sell them anything.

In today's digital world, dealers simply cannot afford to operate this way. We are dealing with a society demanding "I want it right and I want it right now". As a group, we are no longer patient in dealing with long sales processes, wait times and poor service. I would characterize my personality as fairly even keeled- neither patient nor impatient- however, in recent years I find myself wanting faster downloads and the ease of bundled services.

The "I want it now" online buying habit of consumers and access to the digital global marketplace are big reasons why many franchise dealers now hold on to more of their nicer trade-in's, regardless of the mileage. This practice, in turn, has made it tougher on independent dealers to locate good used inventory.

I grew up in Daytona Beach, FL, working in the family businesses. This was a lifestyle, not a choice. In my grandfather's opinion you worked and you went to school (in that order). I learned at a young age the importance of being consistent, providing a valuable service at a fair price, and most of all, providing great customer service. Until 1993, one of my family's primary businesses was operating four independent hotels on Daytona Beach; nowhere did the importance of a satisfied customer ever become more evident to me, than during these years. Like at the company I work for now there were no term contract agreements and no long term commitments from the customers for our business to rest its laurels on. It was all about creating personal relationships and making sure the customers felt they received great service for their money! If the customers are happy they will be back next year to stay with you again. Otherwise, you can bet they not only book elsewhere, but will also tell others about the less than perfect experience they had.

Applying this philosophy later in life I found myself running two franchise stores in rural Georgia with 6 product lines and two separate used car lots all in different towns. Keeping up with the day to day operation was challenging to say the least, with much of the challenge coming from within. The car business is so multi-faceted that it attracts dealers from all backgrounds and walks of life. Some dealers come from a sales background, auto parts and service, accounting, finance and so on. Like many people drawn to the car business, for me it was a passion for automobiles and a love for sales. As humans we tend to gravitate towards areas of strength or interest. Because of this it's easy to not pay attention to areas of disinterest, but that's when glaring black holes begin to appear that you may not readily be able to see. Sometimes you just need to take a step back and take stock of everything going on. For me coming from a strong car sales background my Achilles heel was the parts and service department. My sales CSI ratings at both franchise locations were among the top in the region; however my service CSI was running in the bottom half of the pack, and I wondered why? This only became evident to me when the manufacturer was warning us that we may not receive some extra incentive money unless we improved this area. I knew the importance of keeping customers satisfied and I felt that we made this a priority, so it was perplexing. Numbers looked good, ticket count was better than average, employees seemed generally happy, no major customer complaints (that made it to me anyway)?? I began having meetings with the service writers and parts counter workers, the mechanics and of course the service managers who were facing the brunt of the blame. It was agreed with my business partners that I needed to hire a consultant for $5,000.00 plus expenses to provide us an assessment. The consultant quickly pointed out some minor issues and made recommendations for fixes. The main recommendation was an easy one albeit hard for me to swallow. In his opinion it appeared that I didn't pay enough attention to my service and parts departments. I couldn't believe what he was telling me. What do you mean I don't pay attention to my business? I make it a point to say hello to everyone each morning and goodbye each night, even meet with the service and parts managers once a week to go over concerns and listen to suggestions. As I was denying the accusation verbally, silently in my head in another part of my brain there was a calculator tabulating the amount of actual time I spent in the service department even the amount of time I spent just thinking about service in comparison to sales and administration. It was miniscule.

This was a failure that I had to embrace and rectify. So I began spending 3 mornings a week in the service department waiting on customers and assisting with service writing while interacting with the technicians and parts department. So without spending any additional money on advertising or performance bonus programs, just by paying real attention and being personally involved things improved. Of course for the most part as an independent dealer no one is standing over you prepared to call you out on a bad CSI score, but it doesn't make it any less important. To me a CSI rating is like taking the temperature of your business. Let's face it, if your customers are not happy, similarly to the hotel customers of my youth, they will not only go elsewhere, but will also certainly be telling others about their unsatisfactory experience. In contrast to the hotel guests of the 80's and early 90's, today's customers use not only local word of mouth, but also technological tools, including social media and real-time reviews of sites such as Angie's list to voice their dissatisfaction. At our used car lots we had a comment card box, and each customer was given a comment card at delivery to fill out if they so chose. We also provided an email address that went straight to myself and the comptroller and encouraged customers and employees to let us know their opinion both good and bad. Then we would do follow up calls (just like at the franchise store) to ensure the customer was satisfied with their experience.

Trust but verify

The term "trust but verify" is widely used in business but let me tell you I learned the hard way more than once just how important this statement is. Online job search sites are a great way to find new employees. Like everything else on the internet though, don't believe everything you read. In a dealership there is ample opportunity for you as an owner to be taken advantage of by an employee. From a customer service standpoint, your employees are the face of your dealership and regardless of their role they are interacting with your customers on some level. I cannot stress enough how important it is when hiring to verify previous employment, run a background check and, if your insurance company doesn't already run a driver's license history do it yourself. Also create and require your employees sign an employee handbook spelling out how your company expects the employee to conduct themselves and treat your customers. Further it's a good practice to have at least one of your employees other than a manager in the new hire interview. Feedback from a current productive employee provides good insight into how this new personality will work with your other staff. Don't be selective with verifications in your hiring process (Joe seems like a nice fella he's not the type that would do anything wrong?? Bob says he was a great salesman when he worked with him at the ford store 5 years ago, Bobs been here 3 months and sold 30 cars so he would know) do it for everybody no matter what the job description. People do a lot of bad things in their lives, and I have found the car business to be a magnet for many of these characters. I am not an attorney and I don't give legal advice. This is an observation from past experiences: I have found that as long as you as an employer have done proper due diligence in making sure you have created a safe working and shopping environment most times it makes it difficult for the plaintiff's attorney to find the company liable for an employee's misconduct (again there are services out there that can help you with this process, insurance companies can point you to a reputable source).

Now think about your business. Depending on your particular type of operation you may offer indirect lending and have a separate F & I office, or operate as BHPH providing in house financing and depending on the size of your operation you may maintain a related finance company next door or at least employ a finance manager to handle the contracting and ancillary products. In either case there is ample opportunity for you to get taken advantage of. Over my career I have seen and heard of finance directors stealing cash (outright theft, manipulating the down payment actually received from the customer on the paperwork, charging customers for additional services your dealership doesn't actually offer etc.), forging signatures of buyers on paperwork, creating pay stubs, power booking used vehicles before sending a deal to the finance company for approval, and credit fraud. All of which you as the licensed dealer and garage liability insurance policy holder are ultimately responsible for. Or a sales manager's wholesaler friend may be buying trade-ins slightly behind value and then splitting the profit with them or just paying them cash under the table for each purchase. Or, they may be buying vehicles for inventory from wholesalers for a little more than the car is bringing at the auction and then getting rebated under the table. Buying inventory off the street there is also the potential to purchase a vehicle with a fraudulent title that may have been flood damaged or rebuilt and now mysteriously has a clear title. The list goes on and on but it's not just the employees you have to watch out for. It's the customers too.

Consumer title fraud is an all too common occurrence especially on an independent dealer's lot. Crooks naturally assume that an independent dealer does not have access to services like real-time stolen information, and real-time owner and lienholder verifications that are common services available to franchise dealer groups through expensive monthly service fee system integrations. Say a person steals a car in Georgia and drives it to Louisiana where a forger has a fraudulent printed Texas title ready. The thief stops at a local dealership that has "we buy cars" on a sign out by the road. The crook presents the clear fraudulent title and sells the vehicle for full wholesale value or a little less. The dealer then preps the car and puts it out for sale. The vehicle sells the next day, title and registration work is created and a temporary driving permit is placed on the vehicle. The dealer sends his paperwork to the local collector for processing, except when the collector enters the VIN into the state database to create a new titling transaction, it runs a system inquiry check in the background through the National Motor Vehicle Title Information System (NMVTIS) which shows that the vehicle has an active flood brand title in Georgia. The collector informs the dealer that the Texas title they presented was fraudulent and the vehicle was actually a flood car from Georgia. The dealer must then unwind the deal get the title situation straightened out and ultimately lose thousands of dollars on the flood vehicle they now own and can't retail, for free and clear title money.

There is a cost effective web-based option available for finding this information so you don't find yourself stuck. With no monthly fees and on a pay per pull basis independent dealers can have access to the same data that large volume franchise stores do. By simply entering the VIN, a title check of the NMVTIS database delivers current DMV title brand and status, odometer information, real-time stolen information, salvage and total-loss reports from most major insurance companies. Really there is no reason not to have information like this available to you when you need it.

Be active in your associations and community

Most states maintain a local National Independent Automobile Dealers Association (NIADA) affiliated chapter. Honestly when I was a dealer beyond being a member and sending in my annual dues payment I was not active in the association and was not in tune with the goings on regarding proposed laws and rules that could have adversely affected my business. Now that I am a vendor and involved with several IADA's I can't count the number of potential adverse actions the local and national association chapters have prevented from becoming relevant! Having a cohesive informed group that can lobby legislators and government regulators on behalf of the industry is a huge benefit that you may be overlooking.

The continuing education offered through most associations to its members and non-members is always up to date and cost effective. At these education sessions expert trainers are on hand to answer any questions you may have. The affiliated association events such as local town hall meetings, education seminars, auction drives, and national conventions afford you the opportunity to mingle with the best operators, speakers, and industry vendors.

One association event in particular that our company has sponsored and that I have participated in for the past few years is the NIADA leadership conference in Washington D.C. At this event NIADA puts top officials from all the regulatory agencies who have purview over the automobile and finance industry in a room before independent dealers from around the country. I participated in the "Day on Capitol Hill" where NIADA lobbyists set up meetings with both Democrat and Republican House and Senate leadership with small groups of dealers and associated industry partners. It was eye opening for me to see just how uninformed federal legislators were to the existence and relevance of the independent automobile dealer industry. Many of the dealers I spoke with who have attended this event got a lot out of it and I highly suggest checking it out. Without dealer involvement events like these that can really make a difference are just not possible.

If you simply do not have time to attend any of these events, national and state associations maintain websites with member links to all sorts of webinars, training, vendors and industry news.

Thinking back on traffic generating campaigns I remember a fair percentage of advertising dollars used in support of local community organizations and fund raisers. To defray costs we would partner with non-auto dealer local businesses. Supporting a local food bank or police athletic league etc. really showed the business in a positive light with the local community. After all these are the people we are doing business with. Talk about a customer service boost! Offering to donate money to the cause for every car sold in that month was a good touch. We used to get the local newspaper to write a special community interest article and mention the sponsor's names or location of the event without cost. I also found that if you as the owner physically participated in the event it really went a long way.

With changes occurring at such a rapid pace, it's important to utilize all of the resources at your disposal. Even on a tight budget there are things you can do to enhance your business without spending a lot of money. Sometimes this may mean modifying a certain practice or paying attention to the trade magazines and news articles to keep up with the issues, or simply joining your dealer association and attending a few meetings. One thing is for sure. Dealers who watch their business, take care of their customers, use technology as a tool, and remain constantly on the lookout for new opportunities will be prepared to survive when times get tough.

BIO: MICHAEL SAMAAN
Dealer Services Manager
Auto Data Direct, Inc.

Michael Samaan's passion for cars has fueled his life-long career in the automobile industry. Michael began as a dealer wholesaling from auction to auction and selling cars from his family's independent auto dealership in Daytona Beach, Florida while still in high school. After starting college at Stetson University in Deland, FL, his interests turned to the franchise side of the business and he began working for the local BMW Mazda Volkswagen dealership in Daytona Beach, buying and selling their used vehicle inventory and learning the leasing, financing and new vehicle retail side of the business. He later moved to a manufacturer-owned Ford franchise in Palm Coast, FL and served as its used car manager, and later as sales manager. Working in franchise dealerships allowed him to receive several years of manufacturer and industry sales and service training which had afforded him the opportunity to become a dealer principal. He purchased his first new vehicle franchise in South Georgia and after attending the Daimler Chrysler Dealer Academy in Auburn Hills, MI, he continued to gain experience with management of six franchise lines, two used car dealerships, and a rental operation with locations in four cities.

He joined Auto Data Direct, Inc., (ADD) in 2009 as Dealer Services Manager and works with thousands of dealers nationwide to provide a suite of web-based tools aimed at improving their business efficiency in a cost-effective manner. Michael works closely with both State and National Dealer Associations and believes strongly in promoting the importance of dealer association membership and industry education. ADD's wide range of services for automobile dealers includes electronic temporary registration (temporary tags) in Florida, electronic lien and title services nationally, real-time access to motor vehicle registration and title information in 30 states, and access to the National Motor Vehicle Information and Title System (NMVTIS.)

Michael, his wife Christine, and daughter Sarah live in Tallahassee, Florida, where ADD is headquartered.

Contact Information:
Michael Samaan
Auto Data Direct, Inc.
1379 Cross Creek Cir.
Tallahassee, Florida 32301
Phone: 850-877-8804
Email: msamaan@add123.com

In today's competitive marketplace, independent dealers need every edge they can get. Speed and access to the right information can make all the difference at the finish line.

Auto Data Direct (ADD) offers dealers a single-source, web-based solution to work smarter, faster, and more efficiently. ADD's dealer tools put real-time data, paperless lien processing, low-cost vehicle history reports and more right at your fingertips, giving you that competitive edge.

Visit **ADD123.com** and see why thousands of dealers use ADD's time- and cost-saving services.

Use promo code CIADA14 at sign up and receive free account activation!

Take advantage of ADD's great dealer tools and services:

- Electronic Lien and Title (ELT) Services
- DMV123 Real-Time Owner and Lienholder Search
- National Motor Vehicle Title Information System (NMVTIS) vehicle history reports
- Dealer Management System (DMS) integration
- Federal Total Loss/Salvage Vehicle Reporting

AutoDataDirect, Inc.

1.866.923.3123

CHAPTER SEVEN

Definiteness of Purpose

By Tim Byrd

I grew up in south Mississippi as the grandson of a sharecropper. My dad was a well-established business owner by the time I was born as I am the youngest of six kids. He opened one of the first supermarkets in the south, and from the time I was old enough to walk, I was carrying out boxes, bagging groceries and stocking shelves. Always studying how to better himself and his business, my Dad traveled to various shows and conventions checking out the latest grocery store technology and picking up many ideas that we still see in grocery stores today. I remember having cash registers that had cranks on them so when we lost electricity we could just punch in the food prices, turn the crank and add up the grocery bill. Later, laser scanners, bar codes and moving conveyer belts improved the cashier's life greatly. Purportedly, my father's store was one of the first stores anywhere to have grocery carts, or "buggies," as we called them.

Just as my brothers and sisters before me, and I'm sure like many of you who grew up in a family business, I wanted nothing to do with the grocery business. All of my siblings managed to eventually graduate from college and go on to have successful careers in various fields of endeavor. I, however, being the youngest and having the mentality of *Dennis the Menace*, fumbled and bumbled through my youth. I tried college; it wasn't for me. I tried the military where I learned a lot and experienced things I would not have otherwise, but I had no intentions of making that my career.

After my military service, I moved to Virginia where I had been stationed and went to work as a door-to-door life insurance salesman. 100% commission- a baptism by fire. I began reading "self help" books. This is where my education truly began. After a couple of years of knocking on doors with "Hi, my name is Tim Byrd. I was in the neighborhood and thought I would stop by and introduce myself. Have you thought about what your family will do if something should happen to you? I'm not trying to back the hearse up to the door, but if you have not planned for that, now would be a good time to sit down and make sure your loved ones are taken care of in the event of your untimely death." Cheesy, huh? However, it worked well enough to keep me fed. After a couple of years, a friend of mine I had worked with selling insurance, moved over to the car business and told me that "the customers come to you". No more knocking on doors? They come to you? I thought maybe this was the place for me. So, I followed and soon found myself as a Toyota / Volvo salesperson. Of course, it wasn't quite as easy as he described. Which helped me understand one of life's simple truths: "nothing worthwhile is easy". The car business is one of the only businesses that, still today, it does not matter your background, but your level of desire to succeed. That drove me to study more of the self-help books.

Remember the book by Napoleon Hill, Think And Grow Rich? What an eye opener for me. In this book, Napoleon Hill outlined seventeen principles for success, the first of which was Definiteness of Purpose. This chapter revisits Definiteness of Purpose and other lessons I have learned along my 30+-year journey in sales, primarily because in sales it is vital to have a clear vision, knowing your "why" in order to reach your potential.

"Whatever the mind can conceive and believe, the mind can achieve." - Andrew Carnegie

As Napoleon Hill points out, there is no mention of formal education in this statement. Thomas A. Edison, certainly one of our greatest inventors, with only three months of common school education, conceived of being an inventor.

Chuck Swindoll, one of my favorite ministers, wrote about attitude. His description of how attitude can shape everything we do and how it ties in perfectly with Napoleon Hill's Definiteness of Purpose seems an unstoppable combination worth noting by all people:

The longer I live, the more I realize the impact of attitude on life. Attitude, to me, is more important than facts. It is more important than the past, than education, than money, than circumstances, than failures, than successes, than what other people think or say or do. It is more important than appearance, giftedness, or skill. It will make or break a company ... a church ... a home. The remarkable thing is we have a choice every day regarding the attitude we will embrace for that day. We cannot change the inevitable. The only thing we can do is play on the one string we have, and that is our attitude ... I am convinced that life is 10% what happens to me, and 90% how I react to it. And so it is with you ... we are in charge of our Attitudes.
- Charles Swindoll

Now, I am not discounting education. My point, along with Hill and Swindoll, is there are more important things than mere education. Education without purpose, without the WHY, or without the right attitude, doesn't amount to much.

There are plenty of educated idiots in the world.

The point, if you are willing to accept it, is that God has created within us an incredible mind. It is a gift from God and is the only thing in which we have full unchallengeable control and direction. If you believe you are dumb or poor, you are directing your mind to believe these things. Andrew Carnegie said that whatever your mind feeds upon, your mind attracts to you. This is why it is so very important to understand that all success begins with Definiteness of Purpose. One should have a clear picture in his/her mind as to exactly what one wants out of this life and remind oneself of that goal daily.

Andrew Carnegie said, *Everyone, comes to the earth with the gift of mind power and directing it to whatever they may choose, but everyone brings with them at birth the equivalent of two sealed envelopes. One of which is clearly labeled "The riches you may enjoy if you take possession of your own mind and direct it to ends of your own choice." And the other is labeled "The penalties you must pay if you neglect to take possession of your mind and direct it." Carnegie then revealed the contents of those envelopes.*

In the one that is labeled **Riches** *was this list of blessings:*
1. *Sound Health*
2. *Peace of Mind*
3. *A labor of Love of Your Own Choice*
4. *Freedom from Fear and Worry*
5. *A Positive Mental Attitude*
6. *Material Riches of Your Own Choice and Quantity*

In the other envelope labeled **Penalties**:
The prices one must pay for neglecting to take possession of one's own mind:
1. *Ill Health*
2. *Fear and Worry*
3. *Indecision and Doubt*
4. *Frustration and Discouragement Throughout Life*
5. *Poverty and Want*
6. *Evils such as Envy, Greed, Jealously, Hatred, Anger and Superstition*

Which envelope have you opened? Do not despair if you opened the **Penalties** envelope. It is not too late to throw that one down and pick up the **Riches** envelope.

As a Christian, one thing I have found is that with a personal relationship with Christ, I always have Him with which to share my burdens. It is amazing how peaceful your life can become when starting everything with prayer. You may or may not realize it, but everything we possess belongs to God. We have simply been given stewardship over it.

Chris Patton, third generation dealer of the Mike Patton Auto Family, explains how they view stewardship:

The Mike Patton Auto Family seeks to honor God by impacting the lives of our employees, customers, and community.

He explains, *We believe that God owns this business and we are simply His stewards of it for a season. We want to make sure that all we do in and through the business honors Him. By the same token, we do not want to do anything that will dishonor Him.*

So, we know that God has given us an incredible mind through which we can achieve anything we can conceive. 2 Timothy 1:7 tells us:

For God has not given us the spirit of fear; but of power, and of love, and of a sound mind.

A sound mind along with a positive attitude and the knowledge that we are stewards only for a season is a great foundation on which to stand. In Matthew 25:14-29, Jesus tells a story that brings to light what He expects us to do with what we have been given, i.e., our "talents".

The Parable of the Talents

14 For it will be like a man going on a journey, who called his servants and entrusted to them his property. 15 To one he gave five talents, to another two, to another one, to each according to his ability. Then he went away. 16 He who had received the five talents went at once and traded with them, and he made five talents more. 17 So also he who had the two talents made two talents more. 18 But he who had received the one talent went and dug in the ground and hid his master's money. 19 Now after a long time the master of those servants came and settled accounts with them. 20 And he who had received the five talents came forward, bringing five talents more, saying, 'Master, you delivered to me five talents; here I have made five talents more.' 21 His master said to him, 'Well done, good and faithful servant. You have been faithful over a little; I will set you over much. Enter into the joy of your master.' 22 And he also who had the two talents came forward, saying, 'Master, you delivered to me two talents; here I have made two talents more.' 23 His master said to him, 'Well done, good and faithful servant. You have been faithful over a little; I will set you over much. Enter into the joy of your master.' 24 He also who had received the one talent came forward, saying, 'Master, I knew you to be a hard man, reaping where you did not sow, and gathering where you scattered no seed, 25 so I was afraid, and I went and hid your talent in the ground. Here you have what is yours.' 26 But his master answered him, 'you wicked and slothful servant! You knew that I reap where I have not sown and gather where I scattered no seed? 27 Then you ought to have invested my money with the bankers, and at my coming I should have received what was my own with interest. 28 So take the talent from him and give it to him who has the ten talents. 29 For to everyone who has will more be given, and he will have an abundance. But from the one who has not, even what he has will be taken away.

As you can see, we are all given different abilities or "talents" upon which we are expected to expound.

The person I would say that has had the most influence on me is Zig Ziglar, well, except for Christ, whom impacted every one of the great men I have mentioned here.

Some time along the way I learned from Ziglar that if you want to be a millionaire, you don't go to a guy that makes $50,000 a year and ask how he does it. I am certainly not here to teach you to be a millionaire, but rather about some of the things that helped me to be successful. Ziglar defines success as:

Success means doing the best we can with what we have. Success is in the doing, not the getting, in the trying, not the triumph. Success is a personal standard, reaching for the highest that is in us, becoming all that we can be.

I think the most important things for me on a daily basis are prayer, studying God's word and seeking motivation from various sources.
Ziglar pointed out so much in the way of motivation that has and continues to inspire me daily.

After Zig Ziglar's death (which I must admit I cried, like with the loss of an old friend) author Henrik Edberg wrote a blog that highlighted some of Ziglar's timeless motivational quotes.

1. You have to keep the motivation up.
"People often say that motivation doesn't last. Well, neither does bathing – that's why we recommend it daily."

This is so true for many things in life. It's not like you can hit a light switch and then you are changed for life. The most meaningful and important things tend to need continued effort. Now, if you want to start your day with getting your motivation up, here are two quick tips:

- Spend 3 minutes remembering your successes. If you lose your motivation or it is low in the morning then it is easy to get stuck looking at your failures and so you get stuck in inaction. Instead, sit down for three minutes and remember your successes. Let them wash over you and refuel your inspiration and motivation.

- Make a list of upsides. Take a few minutes to write down all the benefits you will get from achieving something, for example, getting into better shape or making more money. Be sure to include very personal reasons and benefits, like being able to travel to your dream destination or spending more quality time with your son or daughter. Put that list somewhere that you will see it every day until you reach your dream.

2. Failure is not permanent.
"Remember that failure is an event, not a person."

It is very easy to start thinking of mistakes or failures like permanent things. Like they are you and you are a failure or loser, but these things are just like successes, not permanent. Things go up and down.

Don't identify with the failure. Take some time to accept that it happened, but try not to beat yourself up about it or make it bigger than it is. You don't have to be perfect. And no one who tries to go outside of his or her comfort zone can avoid failures, mistakes and low points.

And remember…

3. Learn what you can from your low points.
"If you learn from defeat, you haven't really lost."

You only lose when you give up and go home or when you don't learn anything from a defeat. If you keep going despite bumps in the road and temporary defeats, then you are still on your way towards your dream and goal. Don't revisit the past too much, instead, learn what you can from the defeat and keep moving forward.

Ask yourself:
- What can I learn from this?
- What do I need to do or not do to avoid winding up in the same negative situation again?
- And what is the hidden opportunity within this situation? (There often is one if you just take a little time to look for it)

4. Look at your world and the people in it through an open and positive lens.
"The way you see people is the way you treat them."
And the way you treat them is the way they tend to treat you. Now, you may not become best friends or get along splendidly with everyone. But with a positive and open attitude towards the world and the people you meet and know, you'll feel more inclined to listen, get to know them better and to help out if you can. Over time, things tend to even out; you get back what you give.

For more openness and positivity towards others, try these two questions:
- What parts of this person can I see in myself?
- How is he or she like me?

This can help you shift your perspective from what is different about us to what the two of you have in common. It tears down the mental barriers between the two of you and you can feel closer to and more understanding and appreciative of this person.

5. Get the ball rolling today.

"If you wait until all the lights are "green" before you leave home, you'll never get started on your trip to the top."

You can wait for everything to be just perfect before you get started, but that usually results in years passing you by before you get going or you may never get started at all.

Beginning something can of course be scary and uncomfortable as you step into the unknown.
Henrik Edberg

I did not sell cars very long. I must admit that picking through the squirrels was a most difficult and frustrating task. Once I finally landed them on a car, it was at negotiation that I had the most skill. My knowledge and previous experience in insurance led me to become an F&I (Finance and Insurance) manager. I found that I was really good at F&I. So good in fact, that eventually, after seven years, I was hired to train F&I managers. I was pretty good at that, too; so, in 1994 I took a huge risk and started my own company, Tim Byrd & Associates, Inc.

Trying to get the business off the ground, my family and I almost starved. Car dealers are such a difficult group with which to break the ice; in fact, I almost gave up. The short story I am about to relay is certainly proof of the things I have previously written.

As Zig Ziglar stated *"If you wait until all the lights are "green" before you leave home, you'll never get started on your trip to the top."* Well, I didn't wait. In fact, I dove right in, maybe not the smartest move. I was married with an eight year old, a two year old and a two month old. My wife was not employed and was certain that our next home would be a cardboard box on a sidewalk somewhere. I was beginning to think maybe she was right. I was certainly discouraged. One wintry day in January, three months after I started my company, I was in the garage reading the automotive news classifieds thinking it was probably best if I found a job working for someone else. I walked over to the door and as I looked out across the yard I noticed a squirrel crawling out on the very end of a limb, the tiniest limb, more like a twig, trying to reach a nut at the very end. I remember reading a quote from Ross Perot:

"Most people give up just when they're about to achieve success. They quit on the one yard line. They give up at the last minute of the game one foot from a winning touchdown."

I looked at that squirrel and thought, that's me. I have been sticking my neck out, putting it all on the line to achieve a dream and here I am about to quit. That day, at that moment, I remembered the words of Andrew Carnegie:

"Whatever the mind can conceive and believe, the mind can achieve."

I remembered the words Winston Churchill spoke, reflecting on Britain and the Allies' triumph over Germany, **"Never Give Up"**!

With renewed determination, I pressed on. And with the daily help of God and a great team, DealerRE, Tim Byrd and Associates, Inc., has through ups and downs grown to be a nationwide company specializing in the creation and management of Dealer-owned Reinsurance Companies for the automobile business. As of this writing, we recently celebrated our **twentieth** year in business.

Why Reinsurance? It's what smart dealers do. It provides the tools necessary to help you be a great dealer, to help keep your customers in reliable transportation and to be the dealer that sells them their next TEN cars. Your customers may not remember the great features on their cars or how much they paid, but they will remember how you treated them!

I have a very unique business model. My company specializes in reinsurance for car dealers, for ALL kinds of car dealers. What is unique about my company is that we work with everything from New Car Franchises to Buy Here Pay Here dealers. We, at DealerRE, work with them all, nationwide.

The reason I am telling you this is because as a frequent featured columnist and expert in this field, I spend a lot of time explaining to car dealers "Why" they should have a reinsurance company. In a nutshell, it comes down to more dealer income and better control. Hopefully, most of you car dealers reading this book already have a reinsurance company. If you don't, stop what you are doing and get that taken care of right away.

Owning a reinsurance company as a car dealer makes sense in so many ways. For months, I have been hinting in my articles of a change that is taking place in reinsurance. As a large volume dealer, if you could put your finger on one issue that you would have on your wish list in regards to your reinsurance company, it is having access to the money that is reserved so that you can invest back into your business, pay down your floor plan, buy another store, build a new service center, etc., sooner rather than later.

The way administrator obligor reinsurance works (which in my opinion is the ONLY way to go), is you begin with a fronting insurance company. When you write a warranty or Vehicle Service Contract, that contract is between the fronting insurance company (also known as the administrator) and the customer. The fronting insurance company issues the policy to the customer and assumes the contingent liability. The premium is ceded to your reinsurance trust account. Until the contract expires, premium reserve is guaranteed by the administrator fronting insurance company to always be available for consumer claims. So, if you write a 12-month service contract, it takes 12 months for it to fully earn out. 72-month contracts will take 72 months, which are the majority of the new vehicle service contracts. The fronting insurance company is also on the hook for all claims that exceed reserve.

Until now, a new car dealer who wrote, for example, $1,000,000 in premium their first year, because of the way contracts earn out, would have access to about $70,000 after the first year and about $250,000 the second year. The dealer can see his reserves increase by around $1,000,000 per year, but can only tap into a small percentage of that.

That is starting to change. With accelerated profit accessibility, the new reinsurance model makes a huge leap in helping dealers with their greatest reinsurance frustration- limited access and poor investment income on reserve.

What could that mean for you? Well, if your loss ratio is estimated at 40% after the first year, under the new reinsurance model, you could access $600,000 instead of $70,000. After the second year, it could be $1.2 million instead of $250,000.

With these new options becoming available, dealer growth and expansion will greatly improve through this proven capital resource.

It may be time to take a closer look at your Dealer-owned Reinsurance Company. Times are changing, even for reinsurance.

For the Buy Here Pay Here (BHPH) dealers, reinsurance helps you provide world-class service without going broke doing it. In fact, you can improve your profit while doing it. Statistics show that one third of failed relationships with customers is over mechanical breakdown. They buy a car, it breaks down, and they cannot afford to fix it. In case you are wondering, in most cases, this is your fault as a dealer. If a BHPH customer financed their car with you for 24 months, serviced the car and made their payments, don't you think it should run for at least 24 months? Now, I am not naive. Cars break. But, don't you be naive. When they break the payments are going to **STOP** unless you fix their cars and get them back on the road! As the saying goes, "Customers don't pay for cars that don't run!"

Consider how much it costs to get a customer in the door the first time. Consider that payments are the lifeblood of the BHPH business. Then if your attitude is still "too bad so sad", your current system is costing you a fortune. **I CAN FIX THAT! How?** My answer can be your answer: Reinsurance.

Reinsurance allows the car dealers to warranty their vehicles by establishing a nationwide mechanism, customer funded, which insures that there are always ample funds available to fix those vehicles... not a third party service contract which costs you in the long run more than the repairs, but your OWN warranty company.

Why not have a system in place that no matter where your customer drives that vehicle, should they breakdown, you have a plan and the money set aside to get them back on the road? The beautiful thing is, with reinsurance, your customer continually and painlessly reserves for the unexpected breakdown. THEY are reserving for it.

For the BHPH dealer, your reinsurance company will provide premium finance for your customer's warranty; therefore, not requiring you to pay the full price of the warranty up front, which would deplete your lending pool.

A pro-rated portion of the cost of the warranty is collected from the customer's payment and forwarded to your reinsurance trust account. This will provide a constant stream of reserve to ensure when problems arise there is a well-funded system in place. Problems are taken care of, your customers stay on the road and they continue making payments.

For you BHPH dealers, there is one more elephant in the room I can remove for you: Lapsed insurance!

There's another one to add to the stack: Lapsed Insurance notifications. Another customer has decided that having insurance is not a priority. Some you can't blame. The premium is higher than their car payment. You have hired a full-time person just to make those calls every day, and for what? To cover your butt, that's what. What if they total the car? They can't afford to pay for a car they no longer have, plus you lose them as a customer, not to mention the loss of the car itself. So, you call them up, "You agreed that you would keep insurance on this car. If you don't have your insurance reinstated right away, we are going to have to repossess your vehicle." But wait, they are paying you like clockwork. PAYMENTS are the LIFEBLOOD of Buy Here Pay Here. Dilemma: do you just overlook the fact that their insurance has lapsed? They're making their car payment. You need them to keep paying, but your collateral is unprotected. So, (this is logical) you pay someone to call them and threaten to repo them if they don't SPEND MONEY WITH SOMEONE ELSE! OR you take a chance. You let them ride, unprotected. You, by the way, are the unprotected one.

The problem begins when the customer allows their coverage to lapse, therefore putting into jeopardy the dealer's or finance company's collateral. Industry research indicates that 50% of most BHPH books of business are uninsured. Customers put an average of $300 into insurance policies that they let lapse within 90 days, essentially throwing away that money. Many dealers have personnel assigned strictly for the purpose of making collection calls for the Insurance Companies who are reaping the financial gains off the dealer's man-hours.

Have you wondered, "Isn't there a better way?"

DealerRE can help you provide a better way. What if you made a deal with your customers? "You pay a little extra each pay period to me. In return, if you total your car or it's stolen and not recovered, I will forgive your debt to me."

That is the definition of **Debt Cancellation Coverage**. You collect the premium with each car payment. You can make it a part of their monthly payment to you or a side note. Debt Cancellation Coverage (DCC) is a solution to relieve the lapsed insurance problem and turn what once was an expensive, never-ending problem into a tremendous profit center. By capturing the money the customer would be spending with the insurance company and ceding it to your Dealer-owned Reinsurance Company, you profit instead of the insurance company.

DCC alleviates the need for you to require full coverage insurance. DCC puts you in control when there are claims. Instead of dealing with the insurance adjusters, you have a professional claims team looking out for your best interest. Nationwide, dealers who offer DCC avoid unprotected collateral on the road and the need to absorb uninsured losses.

Further, DCC makes it simple for you to enroll, right away, your current customer base and your new customers, at time of sale. This is NOT Liability Insurance. The State requires liability. YOU only require your collateral to be covered. Since you require it and you make collection calls on it, doesn't it make sense for you to profit from it? Besides, an added benefit for the customer is that they can usually get DCC and a VSC for less than they can buy insurance alone from that other guy.

Another very important benefit to owning a Dealer-owned reinsurance company is tax benefits.

Your Vehicle Service Contract, DCC, Warranty, and many other reinsurance product reserves can be ceded into YOUR Dealer Reinsurance Trust Account.

I am not a CPA, but I know some good ones. They tell me in layman terms, reinsurance companies are small property and casualty companies. "Small property and casualty insurance companies with less than $1,200,000 in annual net premiums may elect to be taxed only on investment income under Internal Revenue Code 831 (b)." Distributions are taxed at the dividend rate. These corporations, unlike "S corporations" or Limited Liability Corporations (LLC) where income flows through to the shareholders annually, are "C corporations". 831(b) "C corporations" allow the shareholder a more long-term approach. If a distribution is not desirable, you can retain the money in your reinsurance company or you or your other business entities may borrow money from your reinsurance company. 831(b) corporations make great retirement programs. Earned reserve can be invested in stocks, bonds or other securities within the Trust account. 831(b) corporations make a great estate planning tool.

Turnkey, DealerRE sets up the entire program. You, the dealer, get the best of both worlds. You own the company, so what you provide as coverage on your vehicles is an actual warranty, not a service contract. The premium cost for your warranty is ceded into your trust account. Only YOUR premium goes into your account and only YOUR claims are paid out of that account. The great thing is that it doesn't need to be public knowledge that you own the company because the managing agency, along with its expert partners, takes care of EVERYTHING: claims adjudication, accounting, training, ongoing support, etc. All you do is sell more cars. In addition, you can up-sell your own service contract and reap the underwriting profits on that.

Here's an example of how it would work: When you sell a service contract for let's say $1,595, and your dealer cost is $995, your store makes an immediate $600 profit. You then send the $995 into your warranty company. Around $200 goes to overhead/admin cost which is typical of any warranty company, and the remainder, $795, goes into reserve. If you sell 20 per month you would reserve $15,900 per month or $190,800 in a year. Even if you have claims of 50%, you would have $397.50 per contract or $95,400 annually in additional profit. In other words, the sale you used to make $600 profit on, you would now make $997.50. (Now you know why your service contract company loves you so much.) Add to that your certified warranties and you're looking at more like $150,000 in additional profit.

Recap: Selling more cars, turning your inventory faster, making more gross profit per car sold, making additional profit on the sale of service contracts, all the while making the customer smile. Now that's doing the right thing and helping you gain a competitive advantage.

Dealer-Owned Certified, finally a smart approach to certified pre-owned (CPO) for independents.

Every dealer can improve his/her business and profits with reinsurance.

God's mercies are new every morning.

Definiteness of Purpose is renewed every day.

Motivation, like bathing, is recommended daily.

Whatever the mind can conceive and believe, the mind can achieve.

BIO: TIM BYRD
Founder/President
DealerRE, a Tim Byrd & Associates Company

DealerRE is a managing agency located in Gloucester, Virginia, with expertise in Dealer-Owned Reinsurance Companies, BHPH Operations and F&I Development.

The stepping stones that brought Mr. Byrd to his admirable credentials have family beginnings. Even as a youth, he participated in and witnessed his family's grocery business growing to be the largest in several surrounding Southern Mississippi counties. During an era that birthed the Supermarket, Tim was instilled with the old-fashioned traits of persistent hard work and operating by the golden rule. These core values became his persona throughout his tour in the U.S. Coast Guard and subsequent operation of multiple businesses.

Starting in the field of insurance with John Hancock Insurance Co., Mr. Byrd became intrigued with the industry of car sales, deciding to plant his talent in that industry. Over the next several years, his exceptional performance as an F&I Manager led the way for him to become a renowned trainer for other F&I Managers. Tim was armed with the unique combination of "degrees" in insurance, sales, F&I, and servant-leadership ethics.

This talent nearly dictated that he begin his own company, which, for 20 years now, has successfully enhanced scores of dealers' businesses. Today, Tim reports, "Our team's knowledge of every aspect of the car business, combined with our commanding knowledge of reinsurance, allows us to be a trusted source to guide dealers to greater profits, in a simple, secure and successful environment."

Tim has been featured many times in The Virginia Independent News, Special Finance Insider, Around the Commonwealth, DealerELITE.net, The BHPH Report and the Dealer Business Journal. Tim is a sought after speaker and co-author of the **#1 Best Selling book "Unfair Advantage"**.

The same passion for others' business success can be found in Tim's love for his family, including five beautiful children. Tim summarizes, "above all, my passion as a Christian man strives to reflect the values of my Lord and Savior Jesus Christ."

Contact Information:
DealerRE
7319 Martin St. Suite 4
Gloucester, VA 23061
(804) 824-9533
Website: DealerRE.com
2-minute Reinsurance overview Video: WhyReinsurance.com

CHAPTER EIGHT
DISTINGUISHING YOUR BUSINESS by Jumping Off The "Brandwagon"

By David Villa

In this chapter we will look at 5 ways to maximize our branding efforts. Never before has there been such an emphasis on branding than in today's marketplace. The key is getting this right so that we can begin to separate ourselves and our product from all of the others competing for this edge. We are all drawn to the comfort level that brand recognition provides. And provision will be the underlying message as we move through this chapter. Ask anyone in business and they will certainly tout the importance of branding. As a marketer, you can imagine that I am a true believer in branding; that is, a believer in "true" branding. The way we define branding appears to be shifting. The definition that I have adopted is the act of permanently leaving a mark on something. With the emergence of the technological race and our mobile society where choices are at our fingertips it seems as though there is a movement to define branding as just being seen. Everyone seems to be using technology as his/her source of branding, be it social media, YouTube, podcasting or broadcasting. Again, as a marketer I am your biggest cheerleader when it comes to using these amazing tools to promote your business. However, I would encourage you to never mistake being seen with building a brand. This "look at me" approach may get some attention and may even land some business, but the companies that have truly been able to establish winning brands have done one thing really well. They have distinguished themselves.

Successful Branders

Building a brand should never be measured by the amount of advertising that you can throw at the marketplace. Brands are built by offering the marketplace something distinguishable. Consider Harley-Davidson, arguably one of the world's most recognizable brands. What has been so alluring about Harley-Davidson? They compete with world-class motorcycle manufacturers that statistically are more reliable, less expensive, convenient to purchase, and yet, Harley-Davidson leads the world in sales of motorcycles and merchandise. Their brand is known worldwide and has become an American icon. So, what is it that makes their brand so distinguishable? Harley-Davidson has presented something to the public larger than two wheels and an engine. They made a bigger sale years ago that overshadowed their motorcycles; they sold the dream of freedom, the experience of the open roads on an American machine that stood for much more than a motorcycle was capable of.

For those of you who may be looking for a more modern example, please consider Uber- a billion dollar brand that seems to have come out of nowhere. Once again, Uber brings something distinguishable to the marketplace. We no longer have to choose the traditional yellow taxicabs. Uber offers more choices and the convenience of selecting our car and driver right from our mobile phones. The have leveraged new technology to redefine what we have traditionally thought of as taxi services.

The "Brandwagon"

Everyone seems to be jumping on the "brandwagon" and yet most seem only to be attempting to shout the loudest or flail their arms the longest. Maybe it's because most marketers will tell you that branding is about getting your name and your message in front of customers. How we interpret that is where most of us go astray. It's time to evaluate our branding strategies. How can we know if we are on the "brandwagon"? Just take a look around because the "brandwagon" is full. In other words, are you attempting to brand yourself in the usual ways? Are you doing the same things that your competitors are doing to get their name and message out to the marketplace? If so, you're on the same ride. Look to your left and your right and say "hello" to your competing brand. If you are just looking for a little more business you may be ok, but that is not building a brand, that is simply branding.

Branding is more of a fleeting action. Building a brand is a result of creating something larger than your product or service. It's about dinging the marketplace with something that delivers more than the obvious. Identifying what distinguishes you or your company's product or service is the place to start. My recommendation here is not to go for what you think you can pull off or what you think will work, but rather what you would have it look like if there were no obstacles, no barriers, and no preset limitations as to how you could affect your industry. In other words, let your imagination be the only limitation. Surrounding yourself with innovative thinkers is also recommended. Those who not only think outside the box, but who dare to throw the box out the window. Forget what you know about the traditional answers and think boldly about how you can innovate an industry. Years ago you would have been labeled a fool if you tried to bottle water and sell it. This year bottled water will out sell soda. There is story after story and brand after brand that we can acknowledge as game changers, the question is are we good students of history?

Step One: Think Benefits
If I had to narrow down in one word why people purchase a particular product or service, that word would be "benefits". The benefits that the consumer expects to experience are what

trigger the decision to purchase. The benefits that the consumer actually experiences after the purchase are what trigger the decisions to purchase again. Understanding that the benefits are what trigger the purchase allows me to not only create as many possible benefits to offer the consumer, but once again, allows me to create more distinguishable benefits. As the owner of a direct mail marketing company, the mission of my company is to connect drivers with dealers. This is what we are known for. We have evolved from just delivering an invitation in the mail to creating a virtual dealership that our clients can use as a second location. Each day we examine our product and what it is providing to our clients. As our competitors react to our evolution by attempting to dissect our product and offer some type of replication in their own product. By the time our competitors can effectively implement a piece of our current program we have already moved on to the next improvement to provide the client with more benefits. This ongoing process is crucial to our success and embraced by our industry. Obtaining this edge allows us to deliver proposals to the marketplace with the confidence of knowing that our product is not only distinguishable but is the clear choice among our competitors. We have clearly defined our brand as "SMART MAIL".

Step Two: Define Your Brand

Defining your brand can be challenging and should not be taken lightly. Although it's not impossible to make adjustments as you grow, you want to have a clear picture of what your brand will represent. Having to reinvent your brand along the way will prove destructive. Once you identify what you or your company ultimately stands for, you can begin to build your brand. Communicating how you see your brand to those around you, especially your employees is top priority. Everyone needs to be drinking the koolaid. By the way, this is the point of exit if you are looking to jump off of the "brandwagon". The disclaimer is that you will inevitably experience some separation anxiety because you will by design be on the road less traveled (a great sign that you are headed the right direction). This does not mean that we have to reinvent the wheel, in fact, most of us already have a product and or service in place. The key once again is becoming distinguishable by delivering something beyond the obvious. The ability to provide something unique will take you far on this road. Think benefits.

Step Three: Examine Your Product

Examining your product and exploiting all of its capabilities will be an essential part of building your brand. You must analyze it on a deeper level and examine it from top to bottom. All products have limitations, but knowing your product can expose its less apparent capabilities. Become an expert on your product and fully understand its capabilities. This will not only affect how you feel about your product and its value, but more importantly, how you present it. The conviction you have for your product is going to transfer to your customer. What that will look like will be determined by the level of conviction that you obtain. Knowing your product will also allow you to provide solutions for potential customers and solutions are benefits. Benefits are what we are looking for in a product. If possible, consider ways to enhance your product so that it becomes more distinguishable. Remember, throw away the box.

Step Four: Evaluate Your Service

Here we have an incredible opportunity because this is the area that has no limitations. If you are a true entrepreneur this statement should awaken you. Entrepreneurs love to be in control. In control of their destiny that is. Providing amazing service is not only within our control, it is 100% in our control. We can elevate anyone's experience at any time. We can add elements of service at any time. This is by far the easiest and arguably the most effective branding technique available to us. There are many brands that are known for this one area alone. Think about the last great experience that you had as a consumer. Whatever that may have been there is one thing for sure. It's one place that you will find the "be-back" bus. The experience was what branded that particular person or company. We make countless purchase decisions based on the service that we receive from particular people, places or products. Imagine creating such a branding experience that your customers are not only committed to your brand, but consciously choose not to take the risk of going elsewhere for fear of a lesser experience. That is the comfort of provision that great branding brings.

Step Five: Capitalize on Market Trends

Recognizing market trends can prove invaluable when building a brand. Keeping up with current news, social and economic trends allows us to adjust our marketing campaigns to further distinguish our brands. When the well-known "Cash for Clunkers" government assistance campaign rolled out we immediately modified our direct mail pieces to capitalize on the branding created by our government. Monitoring these market trends not only gives us an edge when it comes to getting the attention of the consumer but we are able to leverage the exposure at the expense of virtual ad budgets. We can accomplish the same thing by monetizing trending words, phrases or images. The words and phrases increase exposure through SEO and allow us increased visibility online. This is the one area of marketing where "brandwagoning" may be acceptable. Another area of marketplace trends to capitalize on is the reaction that your competitors are having to economic impacts. When times get tough the general trend is to retreat. This provides an opportunity. Once again, distinguishing your brand by responding to economic shifts differently than your competitors further separates you and or your brand. In times of uncertainty, be certain. When others may be scaling back or slowing down, this is the time to create distance between you and your competitors. If the market is calling for lower prices, don't budge; you may even consider an increase. In challenging times, people look harder at value, not pricing. This is an opportunity to bring more to the consumer. If others are scaling back they will fall short in service as well, especially when compared to your brand as you ramp up your activity. The byproduct of this kind of activity is that it provokes curiosity in your product resulting in more opportunities and at better margins. And when we can thrive in the lean times we will unstoppable in heathy times.

Self-Branding

Self-branding can be viewed from two different perspectives. You could see it as very challenging, after all it's just you, right? I mean really, what can one person possibly do to stand out as the actual brand? Another perspective would be that one person has no boundaries; he/she can literally go any direction. His/her vision can be completely uninhibited by others, creating an unimaginable freedom to brand themselves in their own unique way. Can you guess of which one I may be a fan? I am guessing by the fact that you are reading this book that you are a fan of the second, as I am. This perspective brings absolute freedom when it comes to branding. Your imagination and your actions are your only limitations. There are two distinct challenges that self-branders face. The first is living in the land of obscurity. Even our most popular friends aren't very well know when we consider the vastness of the market place. We will need to jump up and down and wave the flag. The good news is we now live in a time that has made this type of opportunity to be noticed easier than ever. We can literally put ourselves in front of people all over the world with our handheld devices. Everywhere we look there are opportunities to engage with audiences and we are right to take advantage of these amazing opportunities. However, I have to sound the alarm again on this one. Jump! Jump from the "brandwagon". This will be especially challenging for the self-brander. Although we want to sing it, we have to be able to bring it. As equally powerful as the individual attention that we may achieve by marketing, will be the spotlight that is placed on us to deliver. This will be our second biggest challenge. When I spoke earlier about examining your product, as a self-brander you are the bigger part of the product or service that you offer therefore, you will want to examine yourself. What is it that you are willing to do and what are you capable of doing that could be a benefit for your customer? As an individual you can create experiences that only you can bring to the table. You also have the unique ability to tailor the experience moment by moment to maximize the consumer's experience. As I mentioned earlier your only limitations will be determined by your imagination and actions. The action that you take will define your brand. Here's the best news that I can give you. If you get this part right, you will create a successful brand.

Corporate Branding

Corporate branding can be viewed from two different perspectives. You can see it as very challenging. After all, you are relying on a team of people and competing on a stage filled with major players, right? Sound familiar? As you can guess, I am going to migrate to another perspective. Corporately we have huge advantages, more people to lend to our cause (you remember, the ones that you surrounded yourself with that exchanged the box for the koolaid) and typically more resources to help us distinguish ourselves. Leveraging these resources effectively is the difference maker on the corporate level. Cultivating an environment that breeds innovation by encouraging team members to contribute to the overall vision is leveraging the talent that you have. Every team member should be acutely aware of our branding mission and not only be passionate about the pursuit, but also understand the value of his/her role in that pursuit. Avoid hiring those who are looking for a job and search for those who are looking for a purpose.

There is nothing like the feeling of owning a business and having others come along beside you that are driven to accomplish the same goals. Corporate brand building requires one thing that just can't be handicapped. Corporate brand building requires leadership. There is no way around this one. I often hear from clients "I can't do this because I can't get my guys on board". I'm sorry but I want to throw up when I hear that. "Excuse me? Can I speak to a leader please?" Of course, I handle it a little different than that when I am speaking with potential clients but you get the picture. The truth is that they are right. They can't do it. You will find it impossible to build your brand corporately without your staff being on board. This is where leadership is a must. Either we lead effectively or we don't lead. And as a leader you cannot afford to surround yourself with those who will choose moment by moment if they are in or out? Recently, I asked a very successful leader of multi-million dollar company and an amazing brand marketer "What do you say to those who say I can't get my people to buy in?" He replied, "I'm probably not the guy that you want to ask that question to. I would rather do it alone with no staff than have someone on my staff not drinking the koolaid." I agree. The good news is that although at times they will seem elusive, there are plenty of quality people that will recognize the value of a great company and come along side you in your corporate quest.

Brand Loyalty

Brand loyalty is the ultimate recognition of building a brand. Brand loyalty is achieved when the consumer clearly knows that any other choice would provide less of an experience for them. However, the only way that we can gain this competitive edge is to actually have the customer experience that very feeling. Providing that type of product or service is your challenge. My suggestion is jump off the "brandwagon" and begin building your brand. Begin by thinking benefits, defining your brand, examining your product and service, and capitalizing on current market trends. When you see clients that inconvenience themselves or pay more just to take advantage of your product or service you will know you are on the right path.

BIO: DAVID VILLA
Founder and CEO of IPD

David Villa is the founder and CEO of IPD, an automotive marketing firm that services franchised dealerships across the United States. He has 20 years of national sales and executive management experience that he brings to his company. Since the company was established in 1995, Villa has been responsible for pioneering, growing and scaling IPD into one of the nation's leading database management, business development, and intelligent marketing companies in the automotive service industry. Not only is he committed to his business, he is dedicated to his faith, family, and employees. He credits his success to those who he's been privileged enough to call his teammates.

David and his wife of 22 years Diana started Imperial Press Direct from their bedroom in Tampa, Florida. They went from dialing local dealers from their house, to now working with more than 600 dealerships annually. IPD is now one of the leading direct marketing firms in the U.S. servicing the automotive industry. Based out of the greater Tampa Bay area, IPD has been in business, and expanding, for 20 years.

In addition to being the CEO of IPD, Villa is a published motivational speaker. He specializes his training in the arenas of sales, leadership, and team building. Villa is also a host on "Auto Dealer Live," a weekly radio show where dealers go to discuss relevant topics in the automotive industry. Along with the radio show, IPD also has a magazine titled "Dealer Solutions Magazine" that is one of the fastest growing magazines in the automotive industry, devoted to solving dealership problems through quality proof and content.

Contact Information:
David Villa
CEI
Imperial Press Direct

3104 Cherry Palm Drive, Suite 220
Tampa, Florida 33619

Tele: 813.630.5888
Fax: 813.630.1048
Email:David@imperialpressdirect.com

@SERIAL SALES PRO

WHAT WE OFFER

✔ **Sales training solutions**

✔ **Sales tips**

✔ **Sales Strategies**

✔ **Sales & Business Expansion Ideas**

" David Villa delivers passionate, smart and engaging sessions providing a combination of inspiration, motivation, education and entertainment. "

BECOME A SALES PRO!

GET STARTED TODAY BY VISITING:

www.serialsalespro.com

CHAPTER NINE
How The Internet Changes The Way We Do Business

By Chip Cooper

In the early years of our business, prior to the development of the Internet, it was a common practice for our sales representatives to travel several hours across many states in order to meet face-to-face with car dealers and demonstrate our software product at their dealerships. For myself, I would call a dealership and schedule an appointment, make hotel reservations (depending on the distance), pack up my desktop computer and printer, and drive many hours in anticipation of the dealer principal being present and receptive to making an affirmative decision on our wares. It was an expensive, time-consuming process that vastly limited the ground I could cover. Consequently, it was in large part a determining factor on how many dealers to whom I could demonstrate and enroll in our dealership management software product.

Marketing our product in those early years was accomplished in large part by word of mouth. A recommendation from one of our dealers to another was a crucial ingredient in establishing our relationship with a new client and helping build credibility. Later, direct mail became a tool that also played an important role in growth. Purchasing sales lists, creating postcards, and buying postage was effective, but not knowing if the material would end up in the trash can or in the correct hands at the dealership was frustrating. It was much like throwing a handfull of darts at a dartboard and hoping that something sticks.

The development of the Internet forever changed the way we conduct business in ways that were unimaginable before. We routinely do remote software demonstrations over the Internet multiple times a day reaching several states. The physical boundaries once imposed on us have been eliminated; the Internet knows no limits. We now install software and train new dealers directly over the Internet, and as a result, we are able to maximize our marketing efforts and position our product to places that, in the past, were seemingly out of reach. We began our Internet marketing campaign by developing a website for our business. Now, we have a storefront that remains open 24/7 allowing a dealer to visit on his or her own timeframe. Search Engine Optimization (SEO) was a decided factor in ensuring that our own brand and name recognition rose to the top of every search engine available. The next element was to include third party marketing parties in the mix in order to achieve maximum exposure. Cross marketing our website with various state independent automobile dealer association websites allows us to recruit new dealers by permitting them easy (one-click) access and enabling them to connect directly with us. The Internet should serve as an integral piece of your marketing efforts as well, regardless of your business segment. According to a study in 2014 conducted by Cars.com®, roughly 80% of car buyers conducted research online prior to visiting a dealership. Millennials are in large part responsible for this shift in marketing strategy. Here are Six (6) Internet tips to consider before implementing your own online business-marketing plan:

1. Create an effective, responsive website

When you begin building a website for your business, ensure you are able to collaborate with your developer. Whether you elect to use a template website to build on or create your website from scratch, it will be important for you to be involved in the process. While you should be receptive to technical and design advice from your web designer, no one knows how to describe your business and services better than you. Include corporate logos to help create your identity and branding. Whatever your industry, separate yourself from the competition and describe what aspects make you unique and stand out from your competitors. "Keep it Simple" can in many cases be the best approach when it comes to website design. I run across too many websites where it's difficult to ascertain what the company offers. Be descriptive about your products and/or services, but remember to keep it concise; you don't need to write an epistle. Consider utilizing graphics on your site that are mobile friendly. While flash graphics are appealing and are informative on desktop computers, unfortunately, they currently won't display on many smart phones and tablets (notably Apple products). Instead, consider substituting with graphics that display well on both desktops and mobile devices. Additionally, consider a "responsive website design" (RWD). Responsive website designs allow a more favorable experience for your customers as they adapt to most any type of electronic device being used with a minimal amount of re-sizing and scrolling required. Remember the cliché: "A picture is worth a thousand words"? If true, then I can safely conclude that "A video is worth a million words". In our industry, it is a common practice for car dealers to post multiple pictures of their inventory online for public consumption. In my opinion, it is equally important for those same dealers to position video and audio footage of their inventory online to increase exposure and gain a competitive advantage. Don't overlook the impact that video and audio can have on your customers. In the case of automobile dealers, a potential client can now hear the engine purring, and see nearly every angle of the vehicle, while listening to the salesperson walk around and describe all the accoutrements and history of the vehicle. Consider implementing video testimonials about your product and/or services onto your website to distinguish your company from others and solidify credibility. Sites such as Fiverr.com offer a broad range of services including professionally trained actors and actresses that can provide you with video announcements of your company based on scripts that you provide them. The services that sites like Fiverr. com provide are very affordable and can save your company a small fortune in production and videotaping expenses. Video documentaries embedded on your website can captivate your audience and encapsulate everything you need to relay about your company in a concise and effective format. It may just be the determining factor in convincing your customers to purchase your product or services.

Finally, before embarking on building your own website, this author highly recommends that you ensure you maintain ultimate ownership and control of your domain name. Some website developers may attempt to "sell" your domain name back to you, or charge you a fee if you ever decide to divorce yourself from the website developer or company that you have chosen.

2. Search Engine Optimization (SEO)

Remember the 1989 movie, "Field of Dreams," starring Kevin Costner? He played an Iowa farmer who heard voices convincing him to build a baseball diamond in the middle of his cornfield. "If you build it, he will come" was the recurring theme. Costner's character (Ray) embarks on building a baseball diamond on his land and ultimately the ghosts of several great past players begin to emerge on the field. It doesn't work that way when you build your corporate website. Don't expect visitors to flock to your site just because you built it. Your website designer should be well versed in search engine optimization (SEO) registration with all of the leading Internet search engines. While Google still ranks at the top position with respect to search engines, it is important to register your site with others, such as Bing, Yahoo, Ask.com, and AOL, just to name a few. Search engines are programs that search key words in documents on the World Wide Web. Based on the keywords you include on your website, it serves as a medium by which customers can more easily find you. For the older generation, a search engine functions much like the old card catalog system at the library where you would rummage through cards looking for a particular book; once found, the card would tell you exactly where the book could be located in the library. Search engines operate on a similar premise, but they are much more efficient and play a pivotal role in directing traffic and new clients to your website.

3. Third Party Advertising

Depending on your particular business, it may be advantageous to market your products and services across other websites that are well known and correlate with your industry. Our company, for example, arranges websites and marketing feeds on behalf of our automobile dealer base to literally hundreds of different venues. Our philosophy is that while it is crucial for all of our car dealers to maintain a website presence, it is equally important to market their inventory to third party sites such as AutoTrader®, Cars.com®, eBay Motors®, Craigslist, and countless others. Many of the websites that we broadcast to are subscription based and the cost of those services is one that each dealer must factor in their return on investment. Other sites are subscription free and require no fees from the hosting provider. We believe in giving our dealers maximum exposure by marketing their vehicles across as many venues as the dealer chooses to use. In the case of car dealers, when deciding which third party sites make the most sense to post to, they also need to consider the most efficient method of posting their vehicles to all of those sites. In order to reduce the amount of redundant entry on each web site, we make an exporting tool available within our software that transmits the dealers' vehicles with just a few simple clicks to wherever they decide to market. Prior to contracting with your website developer, check to see if they have exporting capabilities that will allow you access to third parties that correlate to your industry. Ultimately, automatic feeds save you and your employees a tremendous amount of time and resources.

4. Social Sites

Social Media sites represent another outlet that allow you to direct additional attention and traffic to your website and attract interest in your product or service. Earlier, I eluded to the importance that we placed on referrals in the early years of our own business, and those referrals have a huge impact to this very day. Social media outlets can function in a similar vein in that they allow your message to be electronically shared and communicated to other followers and users to increase awareness and help establish credibility of your product or services. Broadcasting messages about any upcoming events you may be planning can exponentionally increase interest and participation in your product or service and help build your name recognition. Many of our clients will use social media to promote timely events such as giveaways, raffles, or celebrities that may be in attendance during a special sales event. Promotions such as these may go unnoticed and undetected when strictly limited to and only positioned on your website. Social media allows your message to resonate with consumers in the sense that the information being shared and recommended between users (friends) obstensibly comes from reliable sources and isn't limited to your own contact list. Social media outlets can include, but are not limited to, Facebook, Twitter, LinkedIn, Instagram, Yelp, Google+ and Pinterest. Each venue brings its own sense of uniqueness, style, flavor and outreach to the marketplace. There is a secret to maximizing your exposure and success rate on social media sites and that is to routinely update your social media page with relevant, timely and pertinant information. A Facebook page, for example, that is created without a clear marketing campaign in mind and not routinely maintained with fresh posts and content, can quickly become stale, boring, irrelevant to your base and severely diminish the amount of sharing that occurs, thus limiting your outreach to existing and potential new clients. In the case of your business Facebook page, remember to keep the information salient. Avoid posting, for example, pictures from your most recent family vacation, or your own personal views of a particular topic that are rooted in your political persuasion. Ultimately your business Facebook page needs to remain just that … a business Facebook page. Create and maintain your own personal Facebook page if you need to connect with immediate family and friends and feel the need to voice your political viewpoints. Hashtags, or a (#) symbol in front of a word, are gaining momentum on different social media venues. Basically, when a hashtag is positioned in front of a word or phrase, it turns it into a clickable link. When you click on the link, you will see feeds from your friends or the public about the topic. Hashtags can enable you to further broadcast your message to people who otherwise may not have seen your post. Hashtags can save you time by allowing you to post your content across several different social sites. Avoid the overuse of hashtags as it can diminish what you are attempting to cast a spotlight on. Social sites are another example of a tool that you should avail youself to in order to further your marketing potential.

5. Email Campaigns

Email now serves as an outstanding way to easily, effectively, and inexpensively communicate with your customer base. New product announcements, industry developments, and discount coupons are just a few examples where email marketing can yield huge rewards without a costly investment. We routinely send emails to our clients keeping them informed of recent product releases and developments. We include announcements of integrations into third party partners, industry legal changes that affect our clients, and valuable discounts and coupons to inspire and generate additional sales on ancillary products.

There are several federal requirements and guidelines that any business should know and follow prior to engaging in mass email marketing campaigns. In an effort to discourage and stop Spam emails that wind up in most everyone's inbox, President George W. Bush signed the CAN-SPAM Act into law in 2003 which provides stiff penalties to those that do not follow the rules. There are 7 common sense key components to the law that every business needs to follow: 1) Inform the recipient of whom and where the email is coming, going, and replying. They should all include the person's or business name. 2) Create honesty in the subject line. For example, don't write "Claim your $1,000.00 travel voucher" just to entice someone to open your email that is actually about a new product. 3) Acknowledge that you are sending an advertisement. It isn't required if the recipients of your email list have given you permission to send them emails. It is highly recommended that you obtain permission from your subscribers prior to sending email ads. Reputable third party email companies normally require that you acknowledge that you have permission prior to sending bulk emails. 4) Include your postal address. In addition to signaling that you are a credible business, it also serves as a means by which recipients can "opt out" from future emails. 5) Provide an "opt out" link so your subscribers can easily unsubscribe to future emails. 6) If a subscriber opts-out of your list, you have 10 days to complete the request. Don't charge fees to opt out, don't sell the subscriber's contact information to other companies. 7) Ensure that third party providers are following the rules on your behalf. You are responsible for compliance, even if you subscribe to an email service provider such as "Constant Contact" or "iContact" in order to manage your email campaigns. The Federal Trade Commission has a compliance guide available on its website to assist businesses in complying with the CAN-SPAM act.

6. Analytics and measuring results

All of your internet marketing efforts and expenditures must be analyzed on a routine basis in order to determine the efficiency of your investments. Your efforts may be a resounding hit that introduces you to numerous new customers or they could be a flop that should prompt you to reanalyze your efforts and resources to a more positive venue. Google Analytics can be an invaluable tool in studying traffic movement and involvement in your website. On the "dashboard", Google Analytics outlines the number of visits to your site, page views, average time spent on a page, and other relevant information that keeps you informed of activity on your site.

Your email contact manager (such as Constant Contact, iContact, etc.) can also serve as a barometer by alerting you as to how many and which contacts have opened your emails. It also informs you which email addresses have bounced. Additionally, email contact manager programs are the experts on how to improve your success rate by suggesting attractive tag lines and even the day of the week you should consider sending emails in order to maximize the open rates.

Consider evaluating third party advertising sites on their own merit. Many of the third party sites that our company utilizes notify us that the "lead" is coming from them. In many cases, they may prequalify a lead for us. Anytime a new client is signed up, we ALWAYS ask them how they became informed of us and we keep records. I witness all too many advertising sources that charge an arm and a leg to advertise and promise outstanding results, but they pale in comparison to other marketing venues that don't cost us a dime. Ultimately, you'll need to ascertain which venues are worth your time and resources.

Incorporating the Internet into your business arsenal is not just a good idea, it's a fundamental requirement for any business to compete in today's marketplace.

The Internet, along with the inherent capabilities that it offers, surpasses the wildest dreams that many of us had not too many years ago. It's worth pointing out, however, that the "Internet can giveth, and the Internet can taketh away". Restaurants know this truth all too well. Despite the fact that a restaurant can have an outstanding web presence that includes all the essential ingredients for it to become successful, customer comments on sites such as "Yelp!" can prove devastating if there are consistent low ratings for food quality, staff service, and overall dining experience. On the other hand, customer review sites can steer customers right to you when enough visitors post their positive experiences with your company. Many businesses now rely heavily on social media sites and their impact not only to thrive, but in many cases to survive. Ultimately, your success or failure in business will boil down to how you respond to all of your clients' needs. There's no substitute for a great product coupled with outstanding service. Use the internet to its maximum potential; but don't mistakenly rely on it exclusively to generate new business. Instead, embrace it as a tool that you creatively use in order to reduce your overall operating costs, increase exposure and marketability, and service your customer base. Explore ever changing internet advancements and trends in order to maintain your own competitve advantage.

BIO: BARRY "CHIP" COOPER, JR.
President
Commercial Software, Inc. (ComSoft)

Chip is a second generation President of ComSoft; a family owned and operated dealership management software provider located in Raleigh, NC. Chip grew up in an F&I atmosphere. The car business was standard dinnertime conversation. He has over 35 years experience in the automobile software arena. He works in conjunction with several state independent automobile dealer associations by assisting dealers in the classroom on how to efficiently and profitably operate as well as promote their dealership. He offers solutions to dealers in order to help keep them compliant with both State and Federal regulations.

Chip spearheaded the effort to make the Virginia Independent Automobile Dealers Association (VIADA) copyrighted forms available to dealers in an electronic format for their laser printer utilizing the ComSoft DMS product. Currently, ComSoft is the sole DMS provider that offers the optional use of the Carolinas Independent Automobile Dealers Association (CIADA) copyrighted forms in an electronic format from the dealers' laser printer. Chip continues to reach out to other state associations in order to facilitate their proprietary forms to the dealer's laser printer via the ComSoft program. The cooperative joint venture between ComSoft and independent automobile dealers associations across the country helps to ensure that associations continue to market and sell their forms without the necessity of the traditional, but aging, dot matrix printer.

Chip was born in North Carolina and has been a native of the state his entire life. He graduated Apex High School in 1981 and subsequently attended Western Carolina University from 1981-1985, during which time he interned with ComSoft. Immediately following college, Chip took on full time employment with ComSoft taking on the responsibilities of both building and servicing computers and dot matrix printers. Later, migrating to sales and support, learning every facet of the business prior to becoming Vice President and then assuming his current role as President.

Outside of ComSoft, Chip currently serves on the Executive Committee of the Sons of the American Legion. He is also a member of the American Legion Riders, volunteering in most any capacity that helps to serve both our active and retired military.

Contact Information:
Chip Cooper
ComSoft
Raleigh, NC
www.comsoft.com
919-851-2010 (work)

ComSoft

Dealership Management & Marketing Software Solutions

monymaker™ Dealership Management Software

- ✓ Inventory Management
- ✓ Prospect Management
- ✓ Deal Processing
- ✓ Buy-Here-Pay-Here Tracking
- ✓ Lease-Here-Pay-Here Tracking

- ✓ Compliance Tools
- ✓ Integrates with third parties
- ✓ Quick Books Integration
- ✓ Management Reporting
- ✓ Website Integration

Custom Dealership Website Design

Internet Marketing Feeds

919-851-2010
www.comsoft.com

CHAPTER TEN

How to Out-Experience Your Competition

Learn 4 secrets to creating a business filled with raving fan advocates

By Jonathan Dawson

Anybody can sell a car. Well, at least most people can. Selling a car is not difficult and even making money on a car deal doesn't require much effort. Those two things mostly require following a simple sales process. The real success we want, if we want to race to the finish line, is not simply to sell a customer, but to turn a customer into an advocate.

In this chapter, I hope to inspire and give you step-by-step instructions on how to build a culture that creates raving fan advocates. I will start by defining advocate. Then, I will share with you the 10 benefits of creating them, four methods needed to convert customers into raving fans, and finally, the three simple steps you can implement immediately with your team to start mass producing advocates.

What is an advocate?

verb   advocated, advocating.
1. to speak or write in favor of; recommend publicly: *He advocated that they did business with the salesperson in his review.*
noun
2. a person who speaks or writes in support or defense of a person, cause, etc.: *That customer is an advocate of John.*
synonyms
champion, proponent, backer, supporter, fan

What if we asked ourselves bigger questions than, "How can I sell more cars?" or "How do we make more gross?" What if we asked the really big question: **How do we add so much value to our customers that they become raving fan advocates for us?** What new answers would we come up with and what new solutions to our volume and gross challenges would we discover? You can sell more cars and still lose money, but you can't create advocates and lose money.

Why should we develop a business of advocates anyway? According to Rob Fuggetta, author of the book "Brand Advocates", there are 10 main benefits of developing brand advocates.

Top 10 Things Advocates Will Do For You

1. *Give you referral leads and help sell your products and services, serving as a virtual sales force.*
2. *Write highly positive reviews of your products or services, boosting your online ratings.*
3. *Create glowing testimonials about their experiences with your company or products.*
4. *Answer prospects' questions, overcoming buyers' objections and reducing shopping cart abandonment rates.*
5. *Share your content and offers with their social networks, driving referral leads, clicks, and sales.*
6. *Help you launch new products.*
7. *Create better ads than your high-priced ad agency and more compelling copy than your most skilled wordsmith.*
8. *Defend your cherished company and brand reputation from detractors.*
9. *Alert you to competitive threats and market opportunities.*
10. *Give you profitable ideas and product feedback.*

I will respectfully add to Rob's list the following benefits:

- Advocates willingly pay more.
- Advocates speed up the sales process for themselves and for those they recommend.
- Advocates make selling fun again!

All these reasons create a compelling argument for why you should be focused on advocacy and raving fan development.

Four (4) methods that convert customers into raving fan advocates

Bestselling author, speaker, business and life coach, Tony Robbins, has identified four methods to convert customers into raving fan advocates:

1. Deliver More Than You Promise

Surprise and delight them with added value, and they will reciprocate in kind, sharing stories of your terrific service with their friends and contacts—who are then primed to become your next customers.

2. Move Your Customers to a Better Place

You must empower your staff to take the initiative and make the on-the-spot decisions that inspire lifetime loyalty. You have to create a structure and a system that allows everyone in your organization to consistently meet your customers' needs.

3. Reward Your Best Customers

Remember, the most expensive thing you can do as a business is to acquire a new customer. For most businesses, this takes up most of your time, energy and money, and is one of the hardest things you do. Exceptional discounts, special offers and first-priority status are ways to ensure that you don't lose them to an upstart competitor. Also, your best clients deserve your best offers and personalized communication.

4. Continually Ask Them What They Want

Innovation is essential today. Your business must continue to evolve to effectively meet your customers' needs in unique and powerful ways, or you face the certainty that someone else will rise to that challenge. Figure out how to help them, in ways that they can't help but rave about to others.

Three (3) simple steps to Create Raving Fan advocates for dealerships

So what are the three (3) main methods that cause someone to become an advocate? The primary influencers that you can focus on are incentive, cause, and massive value.

Simple step #1 to drive advocacy: Incentivize.

I remember moving to Minnesota in 2002 and seeing a bumper sticker that I had never seen before. It read, "I heart my Cub." I had no idea what it meant until I went grocery shopping for the first time at local grocery chain, Cub Foods. When I pulled into the parking lot, I noticed that over 50% of the vehicles in the parking lot had a bumper sticker advocating for this grocery store. I had never seen that before. Political groups, religious affiliation, military, schools, and clever sayings – sure, but a grocery store bumper sticker?

Well, it turned out that by having that bumper sticker you could win free groceries and other giveaways sponsored by the grocery chain. Since it started, the campaign has taken on many forms.

As an example, during the promotional period a store employee would go through the store's parking lot looking for a car with a bumper sticker and then make a public announcement over the store's intercom: "The owner of the blue Honda Accord sedan with the license plate GHT-789 has just won $100 dollar gift card for free groceries because they LOVE THEIR CUB!" Announcements like this were made two times a day in all of their locations for a period of several months. This campaign had an amazing viral appeal. Soon thousands of people in the Minneapolis area were sporting a bumper sticker that boasted "I Love My Cub".

How could you take this idea and apply it to your dealership? Here is an example of how I brainstormed with a client to implement a similar loyalty program. It was based on the license plate bracket on the vehicles sold or serviced at the dealership. Black brackets indicate a service customer. Silver colored brackets were customers who purchased a vehicle. Finally, a gold bracket was for loyal customers. Every vehicle that comes into the service drive is immediately identified by the bracket. If no bracket is present, the service customer is asked if they would like to join the loyalty program. Black brackets entitle customers to special benefits such as wash and vac with any service visit upon request, 5% discount on parts, high speed Wi-Fi, and other perks.

At the silver level, the customer receives all of the basic benefits of a service customer and also enjoys increased discounts on parts, service, and future sales. The referral "bird dog" fee is increased for a silver level customer, and the customer is entitled to a complete vehicle detail on their birthday month. Several additional benefits are listed as part of the program.

In order to become a gold level member, a customer had to have purchased more than one vehicle in their household, service them at the dealership, and have referred at least two people who have purchased within the last 12 months. Loyal customer benefits include the following: increased referral fee, a monthly detail available upon request, shuttle/valet service for service pick up, and transport to the local airport. This allows a customer to have their vehicle detailed while they travel and waiting for them when they arrive home.

To create advocates, think of ways to incentivize customers to become raving fans. If a grocery store can get thousands of people to put a bumper sticker on their car, surely a dealership can get everyone who visits them to become a marketing advocate, too. As another idea, why not consider partnering with some local businesses that may be willing to allow you to do some joint-venture marketing? Imagine you sponsored a giveaway for customers who are displaying your bracket on their car: "Attention shoppers, the owner of the blue Honda Accord sedan with the license plate GHT-789 and the ABC Motors Silver Bracket has just won $100 dollar gift card for free groceries because they love their Cub AND they love ABC Motors!"

Checklist for creating raving fan advocates:

1) Unexpected value – What three (3) things do you provide for your customers that no one else in the market provides or that no one else provides at the level you do?

1._____

2._____

3._____

2) Empowered team – Are your team members empowered to "move the customer to a better place" by taking initiative when needed to solve a client's needs? ❏ Yes ❏ No If not, consider implementing a written process that empowers your team to handle minor client concerns with efficiency and expediency.

3) Reward loyalty – What are three (3) things you do to specifically reward your most loyal customers?

1._____

2._____

3._____

4) Continually get feedback – Aside from the (often manipulated) manufacturer mandated New Vehicle Surveys, how often do you solicit feedback from your service customers, used car customers, and unsold prospects?

1. Service customers
❏ Survey ❏ Focus group ❏ Nothing recent ❏ Never have

2. Used car customers
❏ Survey ❏ Focus group ❏ Nothing recent ❏ Never have

3. Unsold customers
❏ Survey ❏ Focus group ❏ Nothing recent ❏ Never have

Simple step #2 for motivating advocacy: "Cause" Marketing
As a motivator, "Cause" Marketing is the opposite of Incentive. Whereas incentive advocates are motivated by "what's in it for me," cause advocates are motivated by "what's in it for others." People become advocates when they get involved in making a difference for someone else. Consider what people will do for something they believe in. People will donate time, money, energy, resources, and emotion for something they care about- for a cause.

Your customers care about more things than a great car deal. And as excited as they sometimes get over the bottom-line, they can become even more passionate over something that is near and dear to their heart. Your dealership probably has many causes in the community that you care about and support. Let's look at a couple of ways that you can give more impact at a higher level and create raving fan advocates who want to support you through a cause.

One of the first cause-based marketing campaigns I ever helped a dealership create was for a dealership in a small rural town in Oklahoma. The dealer was a supporter of practically every booster club, organization, and fundraising effort in his town. While walking through the building, I noticed a wall dedicated to letters, thank you cards, and awards from local groups that he supported.

I asked the owner, "How do you measure the ROI of this support?" His response may be similar to what you are thinking right now, "You can't really measure it, but I don't just do it for the ROI and I'm sure it doesn't hurt us." He recounted several stories of people who had bought over the years and mentioned how much they appreciated the way the store supported a particular cause. I asked him, "What if there was a way for you to give five or 10 times more than you do now and at the same time do so in a way that is measured, tracked and completely self-funded? Would you like to do more?" His response may be similar to what you are thinking right now, "If you can really measure it, I would love to do more and get the ROI."

I asked him to choose a cause that he would like to experiment with that would have a high level impact on the community. He mentioned that he had recently received a letter from the local school district that was operating at a budget deficit sharing a need for new computers for classrooms. Over the next few weeks, we created a "Computers 4 Kids" campaign that allowed everyone who mentioned the fundraiser at the time of purchase to help raise $10,000 towards new computers. When the effort was shared with the school district superintendent, he became excited and asked, "How do we make sure people know about the program?" The answers he came up with were simple and effective.

The superintendent invited the dealer to speak at the next parent / teacher conference. In addition, a letter explaining the program was attached to the paycheck stubs of all the teachers and school support staff. Letters were also sent home with the students. The gist of the letter was, "If you know someone who may be in the market for a vehicle, please send them to ABC Motors and mention the 'Computers 4 Kids' campaign. The school will receive a donation toward a goal of raising $10,000 when anyone who purchases from ABC Motors mentions the campaign." Where did the dealer get the funds for donations? As you may have figured out by now, I suggested to redirect his "bird dog" money from a referral fee to a donation.

The campaign worked really well. The dealership sold 22 cars in the first month and raised over $2,000. The dealer was so pleased with the response that he offered to raise the donation fee from $100 to $200. The following month they sold 35 cars to people who specifically mentioned the "Computers 4 Kids." With a few phone calls from the superintendent to a couple local media outlets, it wasn't long before the dealer's picture was in the paper handing an over-sized check to the school. He was also invited to be interviewed on the radio and the local cable news.

This is called P.S.A. (Public Service Announcement) marketing and it is a wonderful way to leverage "Cause" advocacy. For over a decade I've been helping dealerships leverage "Cause" Marketing. They are able to create advocates by supporting their communities and they get an ROI that self-funds these campaigns.

Individual salespeople can also implement "Cause" Marketing ideas. Recently one of my students conducted a "Car Seat Safety" campaign aimed at teaching the proper installation of car seats and donating car seats. This campaign generated thousands in donations from local businesses, hospitals, and the Kiwanis. The salesperson was featured on the local radio and P.S.A. news spots on the local cable channels. He even has a billboard. He has accomplished all of this as a salesperson on a mission to make a difference. The more he shared the campaign with

his customers, the more advocates he created. His customers now know that he's more than just a car salesman - he's a genuine person who cares and makes a difference. How can your store start creating raving fan advocates using "Cause" Marketing?

Checklist for "Cause" Marketing:
1) Does your dealership actively and intentionally support any causes? ❏ Yes ❏ No
If not, find causes to support or research local charities and organizations you could impact.

2) If you are currently active with a local cause or many causes, brainstorm how you could leverage your referral program to enhance and amplify your impact within your community and self-fund the growth.

Simple step #3 for turning customers into advocates: add MASSIVE value.

There are 2 main factors in delivering MASSIVE value: 1. what you promise 2. what you deliver.

I'm sure you are familiar with the expression to "under-promise, and over-deliver." This concept has been a cornerstone of customer satisfaction for decades. And it certainly seems right. However, in today's competitive market, the one who follows this mantra may under-promise and become underwhelmed with business. Today's consumers are looking for BIG promises and over-the-top delivery on these promises. So to dominate the market, a new mantra must be adopted: "OVER-promise, then OVER-deliver!" To "over-promise" sounds strange and even dangerous. How do you over-promise?

Over-promising is basically making a **big bold claim** about your product or services. Now, obviously this is not for the faint of heart or those who are not committed to creating raving fan advocates! If your products, services, or deliverables are mediocre and you are okay with that, then just go ahead and put this book down, because this was not written for you and you will only frustrate yourself reading it. If, however, you have a unique competitive advantage in how you do business and you are on a mission to develop it into a unique dominating advantage, then let's keep looking at the power of OVER-promising.

Suppose you call a business (hotel, restaurant, car dealership, tree service, etc.) and the person on the other end answers your questions and tells you what you expected to hear. What will you do? Well, depending on how much you need their product and how they are priced, you may make the purchase or you may take the information and shop around. What if instead of what you expected you heard something you didn't expect – a

big, bold promise? For example, let's say a customer calls two dealerships to inquire about a vehicle and receives these two responses:

Dealership (A)
Receptionist answers, *"Thank you for calling ABC Motors, how may I direct your call?"*
The customer answers, *"I'd like to speak to someone in sales, please."*
Receptionist responds, *"My pleasure, please hold for sales."*

Dealership (B)
Receptionist answers, *"Thank you for call XYZ Motors the only place that **guarantees your happiness**, how may I direct your call?"*
The customer answers, *"I'd like to speak to someone in sales, please."*
Receptionist responds, *"My pleasure. My name is Anita and I've been with this company for 7 years. Our sales team is **ranked number one** in our area for **customer satisfaction in a 5 state region**, you are really going to **enjoy working with us**. I'll transfer you now to one of our **certified product specialists**. Don't forget to ask them about our happiness guarantee!"*

That's how an additional 10 seconds can communicate a big, bold promise. This approach will separate you from the others in the marketplace. You may be asking, *"What's the 'Happiness Guarantee' I mentioned"?* It can be as simple as stating that if you are not happy with the quality of your service at any time you can request to speak to the GM or Customer Service and we will listen to and attempt to resolve your concern. If we've missed the mark, we will give you a gift card to a local gas station or restaurant.

Which dealership are you more impressed with? When you "over-promise," it does not mean you promise more than you can deliver. It means you promise over and above what others are willing to do, able to do, or are communicating that they will do. I often discover that companies have stronger and bigger claims they can make but don't adequately share those advantages with their prospective buyers. Why not? In my experience, the market is too competitive to hope someone will give you a chance to do business with you. You have to give them a compelling reason why they should - you have to over-promise!

The second part is to over-deliver on your over-promise. It's not enough to simply make a big, **bold** claim; you have to be able to deliver beyond it! That's right. Once you have promised the moon, you give the stars as a bonus! This unexpected value beyond the expected value is what creates raving fan advocates. This is what triggers the psychological response known as reciprocity. When someone experiences unexpected value, they immediately recognize it as such, and that leads to a sense of obligation (the sense of a debt) and then naturally flows into reciprocity (the sense of repayment). The massive value method to creating raving fan advocates means you are committed to communicating more value than anyone else in the market and then delivering more value than anyone else in the market.

While I was at a dealership recently conducting some in-house training, I took an incoming sales call from a lady named Stephanie who was shopping for a car for her son, Cameron. My objective was not just to set up an appointment (which I did for the next day), but also to create a raving fan advocate. Therefore, my phone techniques sound very different from typical scripts. Once I discovered her objectives, I immediately went into over-promise mode. I stated things like, *"At a typical dealership it's sometimes difficult to get the information you need to make a decision. Here we PROMISE to get you straightforward pricing, including getting you the fair market value on your car, estimated payments, and several options to help you shop and compare. On top of that, I will personally have the salesperson reach out to introduce himself, and confirm the availability of the vehicle and the alternatives to have them waiting for Cameron. Also, on your behalf and for your benefit, when you arrive, you will be introduced to a member of our management team who will ensure the experience meets our First Class Promise. Does that sound helpful?"*

She replied, *"Oh my, yes it does. I have called around to several stores and NOBODY offered me all that help. This is great because I don't like car shopping."*

Phase 1 accomplished: Over-Promise. Now it's time for Phase 2, Over-Deliver! After the call, I made a video introduction with the assigned salesperson, Randy. In the video I introduced him, assured her of my confidence in him and that we would be working together to help her and her son, Cameron. I also informed her that Randy would be sending her another

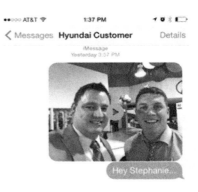

video highlighting our inventory and some of the options we feel may be best suited for her son's needs. But that's not enough! Remember the goal is to create raving fan advocates, which means we'd have to deliver, not just unexpected value, like the

video, but we have to deliver MASSIVE value! Once we found a vehicle that would be a good match, we placed a sign in it saying, "Waiting for Cameron!" We rolled out the red carpet for him. And why not go ahead and add a massive bow on top of the car too, just for good measure. Now let's take a picture of it, add some text to the image, and send a text of the vehicle to mom and son! The end result of our efforts not only looks great, but it creates a sense of reciprocity within the buyer to not only keep their appointment but to want to tell their friends about us. And they haven't even met us yet! This approach is not about a technique, it is about a philosophy of advocacy. It's not simply about teaching your people to learn a word track to get a name and number. I want to inspire salespeople to desire loyal raving fans.

I believe that this is the desire of every salesperson. They want a business of repeat, referral, and self-generated traffic. They want to work by appointments and ultimately to become free from the lot. No one wants to grind out deals, eke out a living, and get by on random ups! And building a raving fan business is guaranteed if you do the things I am sharing with you. You can Out-Experience your competition.

The next day Stephanie came in for her appointment at the promised time and as you can see, mission was accomplished: five star rating! According to Stephanie, "It was by far the best possible buying experience I've ever had in my whole life and I will be telling all of my friends about it." Stories like hers are created intentionally, by design, and with purpose. The reason I teach these ideas is because I am on a mission to create an environment of empowered professionals who are committed to providing an amazing experience to team members, clients, and guests. The end result is that you position yourself to build a client base filled with raving fan advocates who will go out of their way to help you, tell your story, and build your business. Imagine the side effects of such a commitment. Repeat sales? OH YES! Referrals? YOU KNOW IT! Increased profit? Yep! In fact, the speed of sale increases, as does the ease of the sale. The satisfaction on both sides of the transaction also increases. Lots of things go up, but some things go down. Oh yeah, the level of stress salespeople and managers feel goes down and the turnover of your sales staff decreases too.

There are so many really good reasons to build a culture of raving fan advocates. One of my favorite benefits that I love teaching salespeople is how to generate a MASSIVE amount of referrals, and how to self-generate their own traffic. There is nothing quite like teaching a salesperson with less than a year of experience how to self-generate over 50% of his business within 6 months of starting in the car business. Once salespeople learn how easy and fast you can build a referral business through Out-Experiencing the competition, it becomes like an addiction. The veterans are stunned! It's one thing to watch a new person with a great attitude out sell a vet, but to do it by generating more referrals in one month than the vet gets in a quarter or a year?! That's pure magic.

When I ask managers or salespeople, "How many referral leads does the average salesperson collect at the point of sale from any one customer?" The answer is always the same: *"If a salesperson can even get one or a couple per sale that would be great."* That's the typical answer from those who have never been exposed to this new way of thinking and have not been taught how to deliver the MASSIVE value experience. Ask any of my students the same question and the answer you hear is completely different. My students have a goal of a minimum average of 50 collected names and numbers from each sale at delivery. That's right, I said a minimum of 50!

Now do the math! If a 10-unit salesperson collected 50 leads, it would equal 500 new introductions. Those are people whose friend or family member just bought a car within the last month. On average that could lead to 10 appointments, of which 7 will show, and 4 will buy. Now a 10-car salesperson just became a 14-car person without changing any of their qualifying, presenting, or closing skills. This potentiality is incredibly empowering to a salesperson. To discover that they can literally generate leads out of thin air, makes them more confident about their month, their income and their career choice.

Imagine a team that understood this, believed this, and executed this on a daily basis! Imagine a culture committed to creating raving fans. Imagine a customer base that was becoming a support network of advocates. You can do it.

It doesn't happen by accident; it happens on purpose. It happens when you decide that it's not enough to high five a salesperson for selling a car, or for making gross on a deal. It happens when we stop asking how many units did our sales team sell this month, and instead, ask how many referrals did they sell this month? Once you begin to set a new standard for how you measure success in your store it will change everything else, too. How you market, what resources you allocate to referral programs, whether or not you are doing "Cause" Marketing, your pay plan and bonuses, and even how you hire people will change. Everything changes when you are no longer in the car business, or even people business, but in the Raving Fan

Advocate business. Then and only then are you guaranteed to win your race to the finish line!

Checklist for creating a culture of MASSIVE Value:

1) Where can you make three (3) bold promises? Where can you over-promise above the competition? Make a list of possible areas and where in the process you could share them.

Promise #1: _____

Promise #2: _____

Promise #3: _____

2) What are three (3) places you can over-deliver in your customer experience? Pick 3 places where you want customers to say, "WOW! I didn't expect that." And decide how to wow!

Deliver #1: _____

Deliver #2: _____

Deliver #3: _____

3) Do you have a systematic and consistent way of recognizing or rewarding your people for Over-the-top service? ❏ Yes ❏ if not, why not create a recognition and reward program within your store for Raving Fan Service, or MASSIVE Value effort?

If you want to race to the finish line and win the race you have to be committed to OUT-EXPERIENCING your competition. I hope that this chapter has inspired you to do just that by creating a culture of raving fan advocates. I truly believe that we can do this and I see it happening every day in the dealerships that I work with or those that use my online university to teach their team how to out-experience and create advocacy. You can do it, too, and I look forward to hearing how you have implemented the strategies, principles and ideas in this chapter at your dealership. You're at a new starting line in a race. Why not position yourself to dominate it? Thanks and ready, set, GO!

BIO: JONATHAN W. DAWSON
Car Salesman | Trainer | Speaker
Consultant | Coach | Author

Ask Jonathan Dawson what his mission is and you will always get the same answer, "I want to save the world, one salesperson at a time." His passions are: teaching truths that TRANSFORM, coaching that creates CHANGE, and influencing that leaves an IMPACT.

Jonathan is known for his conversational teaching style and common sense approach. Whether he is speaking at a national automotive conferences or writing articles for automotive blogs and magazines, he keeps his information fresh because he is in dealerships every month and he still sells cars. Having been in thousands of dealerships in over a decade across the country, his goal is to help dealerships learn how to "out-experience" their competition by creating a truly unique culture.

His company, LITE Consulting, Inc. provides dealership employees with Sellchology - "Selling through Psychology." This approach is a combination of customer-focused selling, community-driven marketing, and impact-focused leadership

Contact Information:

Cell: (612) 387-7776

Toll Free: (866) 769-8083

Email: jon@sellchology.com

Main site: Sellchology.com

Virtual Training: SellchologyUniversity.com

Facebook: FriendSellchology.com

Twitter: FollowSellchology.com

YouTube: SellchologyTV.com

LinkedIn: ConnectWithSellchology.com

Blog: WhyCarGuy.com

Periscope: @Sellchology

Meerkat: @Sellchology

Speaker & Contributor at:

Digital Dealer Conference

Driving Sales Executive Summit

CBT News Magazine

Six Figure Auto Sales Conference

Social Proof Selling Seminar

30 Sales A Month Seminar

Automotive Super Conference

RocktoberFest Social Marketing Summit

State Association Conventions

OEM Conventions

NADA 20 Groups

NCM 20 Groups

Automotive Blogs

Six Figure Sales Strategies FB Group

Want to Out-Experience YOUR Competition?

If the idea of Out-Experiencing your competition excites you and you want to build a team that thinks and acts in ways that create Raving Fan Advocates, let's build something together!

Sellchology University is a fully interactive virtual training platform that uses multiple styles of learning through video, audio, images, tests, and personal interaction.

- Learn the 4 skills to transform your business:
    1. Psychology of sales and influence
    2. Mastering your mindset and attitude
    3. Connecting and relationship building
    4. Prospecting and self-promotion marketing

- Start creating Raving Fan Advocates today!

- Learn how to get 20 or more referral leads from any one sale

- Learn how to add so much MASSIVE value that prospects will want to do business with you

- Increase your team's confidence and consistency by teaching them how to understand and sell today's customers

Learn more at www.SellchologyUniversity.com
Call (866) 769-8083
Email info@sellchology.com

Selling through Psychology

CONTRIBUTING AUTHORS:

MARTY COATES Co-founder and President, Waymaker Learning Corporation

JASON REAVES President- Wayne Reaves Computer Systems

DAVID CRIBBS Lead Trainer, Auto Dealer University, Co-Host, Auto Dealer Live

JOHN BROWN Executive Director, CIADA

MICHAEL SAMAAN Dealer Services Manager, Auto Data Direct, Inc.

TIM BYRD Founder/President, DealerRE, a Tim Byrd & Associates Company

DAVID VILLA Founder and CEO of IPD

BARRY "CHIP" COOPER, JR. President, Commercial Software, Inc. (ComSoft)

JONATHAN W. DAWSON Car Salesman | Trainer | Speaker | Consultant | Coach | Author

This book is published as a joint project between

WAYMAKER
LEARNING
CORPORATION

To learn more or to order additional copies
of the book, you may contact any of the
contributing authors, CIADA or
Waymaker Learning Corporation.